The Names of
JESUS

The Names of
JESUS

*Over 700 names of Jesus to help you
really know the Lord you love.*

Elmer L. Towns

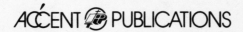ACCENT PUBLICATIONS

ACCENT PUBLICATIONS

12100 West Sixth Avenue
P.O. Box 15337
Denver, Colorado 80215

Copyright © 1987 Accent Publications, Inc.
Printed in the United States of America

Library of Congress Catalog Card Number 87-72819

ISBN 0-89636-243-4

RECOGNITIONS

The chapters in this book were preached as 12 messages at Muskoka Baptist Conference, Canada, during the summer of 1986. Appreciation is extended to Rev. Richard Holiday, Director of the conference for giving me the opportunity to minister the Word of God to over 1,000 delegates each summer.

Also, recognition is extended to Rev. Douglas Porter, Oakville, Ontario, who typed the manuscript from the cassette messages. Rev. Porter was my graduate assistant at Liberty Baptist Theological Seminary, Lynchburg, Virginia, where he earned the M.A. degree. His knowledge of resources on the names of Jesus was invaluable. As we examined the various lists of the names of Jesus in Scripture, we felt many names had been omitted. I want to recognize his diligent search that has produced what I feel is the most complete, available list of the names of Jesus in print.

"Then they that feared the Lord
spake often one to another:
and the Lord hearkened,
and heard it,
and a book of remembrance
was written before him
for them that
feared the Lord,
and that thought
upon his name."

—Malachi 3:16

CONTENTS

PART ONE: OUR LORD JESUS CHRIST

Jesus was a popular name for new baby boys at the time Mary had a son, but within a few decades it became virtually unused because it was special to Christians. Still today it is the sweetest of our Lord's names because it is His personal name.

When people addressed Jesus as Lord in the New Testament, that title demonstrated an attitude of either respect or reverence. But in the early church, Christians were martyred because they affirmed "Jesus is Lord." To them "Lord" meant only one thing — Jesus was the Jehovah of the Old Testament.

Throughout the pages of the Old Testament, the prophets wrote of a coming Messiah who functioned as prophet, priest, and king. The name "Christ" meant "anointed." He was anointed to that office. But He was more than that! Paul revered this office and made it his favorite name of Jesus and the foundation to the Christian's position in grace.

PART TWO: GROUPINGS OF THE NAMES OF JESUS CHRIST

Hidden in the pages of law, history, poetry, and prophecy is a myriad of names and titles of Jesus. He is revealed in every book by type and teaching. Among the many Old Testament prophetic names of Jesus are Shiloh, the Prophet, the Branch, the Desire of all Nations, the Ensign for the Peoples, and *El Shaddai.*

Many of the names of Jesus reveal aspects of His principal work of redeeming the lost. Some of them focus upon His work and, therefore, He is the Redeemer, Saviour, and Mediator. Others call attention primarily to His Person; as such, Jesus is the Lamb of God and the Propitiation for our sins. Still others reveal the mystery of the One who both produces salvation and is Himself our salvation. In this regard, He is the Last Adam, the Second Man, and the Author of Eternal Salvation.

When it comes to naming babies, it seems everybody has some suggestion about a name. It was no different with Jesus. Hundreds of years before He was born, people began calling the Christ child by a variety of names. By the time He was born, He had been called the Dayspring from on High, Wonderful, Counselor, The Mighty God, The Everlasting Father, The Prince of Peace, and Immanuel.

Jesus came not to be served but to serve. As a result, many of His names and titles emphasize His qualities of service. He is the Creator and Sustainer of life. Several names describe Him as the teacher and sovereign of mankind. And then of course there are those names which focus on how He assists us in living the victorious Christian life.

Jesus delighted to call God His Father, and so, it is not surprising there are at least nineteen sonship names of Jesus. Three are particularly important when it comes to understanding who Jesus is. He called Himself "Son of Man," but He was also the Son of God and the only begotten Son.

Several names and titles of Jesus express the uniqueness of His nature and have important theological implications in the study of Christology. These include the Image of God, the Firstborn, the Beloved, the Alpha and Omega, and the *Logos* (Word).

The name *Jehovah* was so revered by the Jews that they never uttered it. It was the name of the One who introduced Himself to Moses as I AM THAT I AM. The proof that Jesus was Jehovah is the fact that He used that divine title in eight ways in the Gospel of John.

Jesus promised He would build His church, and so, one would expect to find Him closely identified with that church. Several names of Christ have special significance in that they reveal His relation to His church. These titles include Bridegroom, Shepherd, Head, Vine, Stone, Temple, and Gardener.

The final book of the New Testament offers the fullest revelation of Jesus Christ in Scripture. It is not surprising, then, that John uses at least seventy-three different names of Jesus to describe important truths about Jesus. This chapter takes a closer look at several of the more significant names in the Revelation.

APPENDIX: THE NAMES OF JESUS CHRIST
IN SCRIPTURE

INTRODUCTION

The Epistle to the Philippians expresses the overwhelming desire of the Apostle Paul: "That I may know him" (Philippians 3:10). Thousands of Christians everywhere have since shared the same sentiment. But Paul and Christians were not the first to long for such an intimate knowledge of God. Many years earlier, Moses had prayed, "Now therefore, I pray thee, if I have found grace in thy sight, show me now thy way, that I may know thee" (Exodus 33:13). God answered that prayer of Moses in an interesting manner: "And the LORD descended in the cloud, and stood with him there, and proclaimed the name of the LORD" (Exodus 34:5).

To really know God, you must get to know Him by name. The names of God in Scripture are really a self-revelation of God in His nature and attributes. The sheer number of such names and titles in Scripture suggests something of the immensity of God. A devout Moslem exhausts his knowledge of his god when he knows the ninety-nine names and attributes of Allah in the Koran. But the Bible identifies more than 700 descriptive names and titles of Jesus Christ. And as Charles Haddon Spurgeon once put it, "God the Father never gave his son a name which he did not deserve." How many of these names do you know and understand?

This book is written to help you get to know Jesus Christ more fully by studying several of His key names and titles. Of course, a volume of this size on the names of Jesus Christ cannot be exhaustive. The author is not even prepared to conclude that the listing of names in the appendix to this volume is exhaustive. But it is an introduction to an important subject, important to those who, like Moses and Paul, desire a more intimate knowledge of the One the angels years ago named "Jesus."

PART ONE
Our Lord Jesus Christ

CHAPTER ONE
THE NAME OF JESUS

"And she shall bring forth a son, and thou shalt call his name JESUS: for he shall save his people from their sins" (Matthew 1:21).

Of the more than 700 names and titles of the Lord Jesus Christ in Scripture, none is perhaps more venerated by Christians than the name "Jesus" itself. A contemporary songwriter acknowledges simply, "There's just something about that name." The very sound of that name is precious in the ears of Christians worldwide. That name has brought about a sense of overwhelming comfort to many in their darkest hours. It is that name most often verbalized in prayer and preaching, in testimony and witnessing. Many relate dramatic, even miraculous experiences of life to the significance of that name.

The name "Jesus" was, at the time of our Lord's earthly sojourn, among the most popular of names selected by parents of Hebrew boys. In the writings of the Jewish historian Josephus, the name identifies at least twenty different men, ten of whom were contemporaries of Jesus Christ. Its popularity was probably to a large extent due to its relationship with one of Israel's great leaders, Joshua, the son of Nun and successor to Moses. In the Egyptian papyri, the name occurs frequently right through the early part of the second century. Then abruptly, both Jews and Christians stopped using "Jesus" as a name for their boys. The Jews did so because it was so closely related to Christianity, which they rigorously opposed and hated. The Christians refused to use the name for opposite reasons. To them, the name was special and held in veneration. It was almost thought sacrilegious that anyone but Jesus should bear that name.

15

THE NAMES OF JESUS

When one reads the New Testament, he must be impressed with how often this name appears. It is by far the most often used name in the Gospels; and, even in the book of Acts, where we see the title "Lord" so often, the use of "Jesus" outnumbers "Lord" three to one. In the Epistles, the name of Jesus continues to occur, though not so often. It formed an intrinsic part of the great Pauline formula by which the apostle often referred to the "Lord" (His Title), "Jesus" (His Name), and "Christ" (His Office).

What is perhaps most surprising about the name "Jesus" is not its use but the absence of its use. With the possible exception of the thief on the cross (Luke 23:42), there is no record of anyone ever addressing Jesus directly by the name "Jesus" during His earthly life and ministry. Further, Jesus Himself apparently used this name to identify Himself only twice, both occasions to persons after His ascension to and glorification in Heaven (cf. Acts 9:5; Revelation 22:16).

THE MEANING OF HIS IDENTIFICATION

In all likelihood, when Mary and Joseph talked to their son, they used their native language and called Him "Yeshua" or "Joshua." If they used the Greek trade language, then they called Him "Jesus," for as we noted previously, "Jesus" is the Greek form of the Hebrew name "Joshua." The name "Joshua" was a contraction of "Jehoshua," meaning "Jehovah the Saviour." It was used to identify several men in the Old Testament, the best known being Joshua the son of Nun, who led Israel into the land of Canaan. Actually, Joshua's given name was "Hoshea," meaning "salvation," and was changed to "Jehoshua" or "Joshua" by Moses, probably when he sent him to spy out the land at Kadesh-barnea (Numbers 13:16).

The name "Jesus/Joshua" is built on the Hebrew verb stem *yasha* meaning "saved." The first use of this verb in Scripture is also the embryonic first mention of the doctrine of salvation (Exodus 14:30). The salvation of Israel is there defined in terms of the destruction of the army of Egypt in the Red Sea. This miracle, so often referred to in the Old Testament, is also a type of the salvation from sin provided by Jesus on the cross.

As borne by Joshua, the name was an expression of faith in what Jehovah could and would do for His people and a testimony to the effect that he, Joshua, was willing to be a part of it. No doubt a major aspect of that salvation was viewed in a military light as the nation went out to destroy the inhabitants of the land and settle it as their own. Still, the spiritual salvation of the nation and its families, individually or corporately, was not overlooked.

Several Bible commentators have noted the typical significance of Joshua which goes far beyond a mere similarity of names. Joshua was the shadow of what Jesus is in reality. This is particularly true in His name. When Jesus was so named by the angel, it was more than simply an expression of the Messianic hope of Israel. It was an affirmation of His real identity and primary concern. "Jesus" means "Jehovah the Saviour," but when applied to our Lord, it is a declaration that *He is Jehovah the Saviour.* It both enshrines and expresses the mystery of His Person and the marvels of His work.

THE MYSTERY OF HIS INCARNATION

In the first mentions of the name of Jesus in Scripture, it is clear that Jesus was more than just another baby boy born to a young Jewish mother. The first to hear His name was Mary who was informed not only that she would bear a son but that she should "call his name JESUS" and that He would also "be called the Son of the Highest" (Luke 1:31,32). When Joseph first heard the name, he was told "that which is conceived in her is of the Holy Ghost" (Matthew 1:20). The name "Jesus," when applied to the virgin-born child of Bethlehem, was an

17

affirmation of who He is, "Jehovah the Saviour."

"Jehovah" was the most venerated name of God in the Old Testament. So careful were the Jews not to violate the fourth commandment that they refused to verbalize this name lest, unknowingly, they were to use it in vain. When they came to read it in their Scriptures, by habit they substituted the name *Adonai,* another name for God in the Old Testament. Because the Hebrew language lacks vowels, words are pronounced as they are learned. But when the pious Jews refused to pronounce the name "Jehovah," people were soon unsure as to the actual pronunciation of it. Most evangelicals apply the vowels of *Adonai* to it and pronounce the name "Jehovah." More critical scholars have chosen to pronounce the name "Yahweh." Actually, because accents and dialects of a language change as that language is used over the years, it is impossible to be certain how Moses first pronounced this name of God when he introduced it to Israel.

To think, that greatly respected "Jehovah" of the Old Testament was "Jesus" in the New Testament! Jehovah Himself became a man. That mystery concerning the incarnation has baffled theologians and Bible students for years, yet it remains a part of human history that one day, the One who made this world and created all things, including the human race, voluntarily chose to become a man without compromising in any way who He was. No wonder that name has such a special significance for Christians. Certainly, if the unsaved Jews were so concerned about using Jehovah's name in vain that they avoided any possibility of doing so, Christians today ought also to reverence and respect the name of Jehovah incarnate, *Jesus,* and never use it in vain as a curse.

When we realize the true nature of Jesus, we have no problem understanding the necessity of the virgin birth. It is not simply an early Christian legend which found its way into the Bible or a novel little miracle to give us yet something else to believe. The virgin birth was the only possible way in which Jehovah could become a man and at the same time remain Jehovah. Jesus needed a human mother to have a human nature, but if He had had a human father, He also would have received the sin nature of His father. With a pair of sinful human parents, it would have been impossible for Him to be the Son of God.

When God created man, He made man holy—that is, without sin. But man's holiness was conditional and ended when Adam fell. Since then, men have been born sinners by nature because they inherited that nature from their father, Adam. "Wherefore, as by one man sin entered into the world, and death by sin; and so death passed upon all men, for that all have sinned" (Romans 5:12). That would also have been the fate of Jesus had He been the physical son of Joseph. In contrast, the Scriptures teach that Christ knew no sin (II Corinthians 5:21), was without sin (Hebrews 4:15), and did no sin (I Peter 2:22).

THE MARVELS OF HIS OCCUPATION

When Joseph learned his legal son would be named "Jesus," he was also told the nature of His work, "For he shall save his people from their sins" (Matthew 1:21). He was the salvation which would also provide salvation for His people. It is not clear that the full nature or extent of that salvation was fully understood at first. Initially, it was widely believed that the salvation provided by Jesus was exclusively for the Jews. This view is evident even in the book of Acts, where Peter is reluctant to go to Cornelius' household and later where the Jerusalem Conference becomes a necessity.

Surprisingly, it was the Samaritans who first recognized the broader extent of the salvation that Jesus would effect. Their understanding of Jesus as "the Christ, the Saviour of the world" (John 4:42), was unheard of in Jewish circles and largely ignored in the early days of the church. One might argue that

19

the extent of the work of Christ was never fully realized in practice even by the church until the Moravian and later Methodist movements, with the possible exception of the evangelistic outreach of the church following the Jerusalem Conference (Acts 15).

THE MAJESTY OF HIS REPUTATION

A name is a reputation. Sometimes one gains a reputation from a name, and at other times a person gives his name a reputation. When I was growing up in Savannah, Georgia, my mother would frequently remind me to live up to my name. "Remember, you're a Towns," she would say. Our family history went back several generations in Georgia and included several prominent medical doctors, one of whom served for a time as governor of our state. As children, my brother, sister, and I were encouraged to live up to the historical reputation of our name.

Just as my mother reminded me to live up to the reputation of my family name, we all need to be reminded to live up to the reputation of the name of Jesus. The Apostle Paul reminded the Jews in Rome that "the name of God is blasphemed among the Gentiles through you" as a result of their inconsistent living (Romans 2:23,24). The same could be said of Christians today. When you behave in a manner inconsistent with the name of Jesus, the unsaved world takes note of your hypocrisy and lowers its estimate of Jesus and Christianity. How many Christians have been reminded of "hypocrites in the church" as they have tried to win their unsaved friends, relatives, associates, and neighbors?

Regardless of the nobility of the name or title ascribed to Jesus in Scripture, He always added something to the reputation of the name. Many Christians today conclude their prayers with the phrase, "in Jesus' name." Sometimes they will cite John 14:13,14 or 16:23 as Biblical authority for that practice.

In those texts Jesus encouraged His disciples to "ask in my name." Actually, to ask in Jesus' name means to ask in His Person and does not mean that every prayer must end with the words "in Jesus' name." Some who pray this way do so wrongly, viewing the mention of Jesus' name as a kind of magical incantation that will guarantee an answer to their prayers. Others use the expression as a constant reminder that when they pray, they do so on the merits of Jesus and not of themselves.

There is a certain power in Jesus' name, however, that transcends our ability to understand it fully. It is a power over demons themselves. Even the Jewish exorcists of the first century recognized this spiritual power and sought to harness it by addressing and commanding demons in Jesus' name (Acts 19:13). The failure of the sons of Sceva to overcome the demons on that occasion emphasized the fact that the name that possesses the power is not the mere recital of a formula but the Person of Jesus Himself. The sons of Sceva did not have a personal relationship with Jesus and, therefore, could not effectively use His name in prayer in order to cast out demons.

Jesus encouraged His disciples to ask for "anything" (John 14:14), including the salvation of unsaved friends, relatives, associates and neighbors, problems in your family or finances, difficult responsibilities, or relationships. The name of Jesus is the "name which is above every name" (Philippians 2:9). Jesus is powerful to save and powerful to keep those who are saved. He alone is powerful enough both to control demons and influence God. We should speak, sing, meditate on, and glory in the name of Jesus. It is even proper to fall in adoration and worship at the name of Jesus (Philippians 2:10).

CONCLUSION

Have you ever noticed how many of your favorite hymns make specific reference to the name of Jesus? Leaf through the average church hymnal, and you will agree that this name has certainly inspired its share of songs. Many of the most familiar hymns referring to our Lord use the name "Jesus." And this is not only a phenomenon among English-speaking Christians. Though pronounced differently in other parts of the world, the name "Jesus" has found a prominent place in the expression of Biblical Christianity, regardless of the linguistic or cultural background of the Christian. Constantly it is sung and preached by those who have come to love the One who first loved them and demonstrated that love from a cross.

Is it any wonder the name of Jesus is so deeply loved by Christians around the world? It is the name that brings us salvation and provides all the assistance we need in facing the struggles of life. It bears witness to the fact that Jehovah the Saviour became a man at a point in history that we might spend eternity with Him in Heaven. It challenges us to come with boldness to the throne of grace in prayer, knowing before we pray that He is there to give the grace we need even before we recognize our need. The songwriter was right: "There is something about that name"!

For Discussion:

1. What does the name Jesus mean? Why was it popular when Joseph and Mary gave it to their Son?
2. Why did parents discontinue naming their sons Jesus? What does this teach us about our attitude toward the name of Jesus?
3. What does it mean to "live up to the name of Jesus"?
4. Should we end our prayers by saying "in Jesus' name"? Why or why not?
5. Name your favorite hymn about Jesus. Why is it your favorite hymn?

CHAPTER TWO
THE TITLE "LORD"

"For unto you is born this day in the city of David a Saviour, which is Christ the Lord" (Luke 2:11).

"Therefore let all the house of Israel know assuredly, that God hath made that same Jesus, whom ye have crucified, both Lord and Christ" (Acts 2:36).

"That if thou shalt confess with thy mouth the Lord Jesus, and shalt believe in thine heart that God hath raised him from the dead, thou shalt be saved" (Romans 10:9).

People change their names as their role in life and office changes. When I began teaching, my students referred to me as "Prof. Towns." Later, after receiving my first doctorate, I began to be called "Dr. Towns." As dean of the B. R. Laken School of Religion, today I am sometimes referred to as "Dean Towns." The changing titles mark changes in my life.

When my children began having children of their own, I thought I was too young to be a grandfather! I told my children not to teach my grandchildren to call me Grandfather, or some cute name like "Poppa." My daughter, not wanting to offend me, taught her daughter to address me as "Dr. Towns." For a while it worked, but the child soon learned that this man was really "Poppa." Also, this little girl noticed that her father often called his father-in-law "Doc." Soon she began addressing me as "Poppa Doc." Although the title was once that of a Haitian dictator, I am now more than pleased to be called "Poppa Doc" by my grandchildren.

Similarly, the name of Jesus has changed over the years as His role and office have changed. In the Gospels, He is most often called "Jesus," although both His title "Lord" and of-

23

fice "Christ" were emphasized at His birth (Luke 2:11). It was not until the book of Acts that the title "Lord" became more commonly used and began to take on the characteristics of a name. When Luke was writing the early history of the church, he chose "Lord" as his narrative name. Probably "Jesus" was considered too familiar to be used and, "Christ" at that time sounded too formal. Another advantage of this title is that it conveyed the idea of relationship. If Jesus is Lord, He is Lord of something or someone.

Jesus is the Lord of your life whether you let Him operate in your life or not. He is by nature the Lord. Ultimately a lord has dominion over one, and the Lord will be the Lord. If He is not recognized as Lord now, He will be someday when every tongue will confess that Jesus Christ is Lord (Philippians 2:11). We may choose to recognize Him as Lord today or be coerced into recognizing Him as Lord at His return.

The normal posture of prayer traditionally practiced by Christians is a symbolic recognition of the lordship of Jesus. As we pray, it is common for us to bow our heads. That is the usual way of approaching the monarch or supreme ruler of a region. That is the way in which we approach the King of kings and Lord of lords. When we bow, we are symbolically showing we owe our allegiance to Him.

THE MEANING OF THIS NAME

In calling Jesus "Lord," a speaker could have been using that term in one of several ways. The Greek word *kurios* is used in the New Testament with reference to an owner (Luke 19:33), one who has disposal of anything (Matthew 12:8), a master to whom service is due (Matthew 6:24), an emperor or king (Acts 25:26; Revelation 17:14), a title of respect for a father (Matthew 21:30), husband (I Peter 3:6), master (Matthew 13:27), ruler (Matthew 27:63), angel (Acts 10:4), a stranger (Acts 16:30), a designation of a pagan idol or deity

(I Corinthians 8:5), as well as a translation of the name of God from the Old Testament: *(Jehovah,* Matthew 4:7; *Adonai,* Matthew 1:22, and *Elohim,* I Peter 1:25). There is no indication that Christians used this term for anyone but Jesus, suggesting it was used as a recognition of His deity.

The translation of Hebrew titles *Jehovah, Adonai,* and *Elohim* by the Greek word *kurios* (Lord) emphasizes that these titles of God in the Old Testament are also to be included in the names of Jesus. The use of the word *kurios* in this way recognizes that several rights belong to Jesus. First, there is the right to respect. This word was commonly used as an address of respect not only to those in authority, such as kings and fathers, but even to strangers. Secondly, there is the right to be served. When one used the title ''Lord,'' it normally expressed a willingness to serve the person or idol so addressed. A third implied right is the right of disposal. As owner, a lord could dispose of his property in any way he saw fit. This is an important concept to remember in the area of our stewardship of the Lord's resources. Finally, the right to rule and hold authority over others is also implied in the name ''lord.''

In the cultural context of that day, a lord had absolute authority over his subjects. When Jesus was called ''Lord'' by Christians, who reserved that word as a title of deity, each of the four above rights were intensified in their experience.

The use of this name is significant in the lives and experience of the disciples, particularly in three instances. When Jesus told Peter to let down his nets, Peter respectfully addressed Jesus as ''Master'' and consented to let down a net (Luke 5:5). That he let down only one net suggests he was doing so merely as a courtesy to Jesus and did not expect to catch anything. Later, when the net broke because of the size of the catch and Peter realized Jesus was more than just another religious teacher, he addressed Jesus as ''Lord'' (Luke 5:8).

A second significant use of this title in the Gospels occurred at the last supper. Again the speech of the disciples betrayed the nature of their faith and true attitude toward Jesus. When Jesus announced that one of the twelve would betray Him that night, the eleven asked, "Lord, is it I?" (Matthew 26:22). Later, Judas also asked but said, "Master, is it I?" (Matthew 26:25). The eleven disciples had come to recognize Jesus as Lord, but for Judas, He was only Master.

The third significant use of this title by a disciple in the Gospels is the time when Thomas answered Jesus' invitation to touch His wounds by crying out, "My Lord and my God" (John 20:28). His affirmation of faith in Jesus as *Jehovah El* of the Old Testament is the apex of the Gospel of John and the highest statement of deity yet attributed to Jesus. John writes his Gospel in such a way as to build to a climax with Thomas' affirmation of the Lordship of Christ. This expression of faith is that of Thomas, the disciples, and—hopefully—you the reader.

"Lord" is the most often used name of Jesus in the book of Acts. It was the name God used of Jesus at the resurrection (Philippians 2:9-11). The lordship of Christ is a post-resurrection emphasis. It was a constant theme in apostolic preaching. "For we preach not ourselves, but Christ Jesus the Lord; and ourselves your servants for Jesus' sake" (II Corinthians 4:5).

THE MESSAGE OF THIS NAME

As is true with each name of Jesus in Scripture, the name "Lord" has a special significance in the life of every Christian. It closely relates to what it means to be a Christian. "That if thou shalt confess with thy mouth the Lord Jesus, and shalt believe in thine heart that God hath raised him from the dead, thou shalt be saved" (Romans 10:9). Some evangelists erroneously argue that this means a person is not saved if his conversion is not accompanied by a dramatic evidence of repentance. Although repentance is as important as faith in conversion, the *evidence* of repentance differs in every experience.

26

If the Lord has convicted an unsaved person about a particular sin and he refuses to repent of that sin, he cannot be saved until he is willing to recognize the Lord Jesus in that area. Often, however, it is not until after a person is saved that he is convicted by the Holy Spirit of sin in his life. This presence of sin does not mean that Jesus is not his Saviour, only that Jesus is not recognized as his Lord.

Recognizing the "Lordship of Christ" is a work of the Holy Spirit in our life. "No man can say that Jesus is the Lord, but by the Holy Ghost" (I Corinthians 12:3). All Christians at some point in their walk with God need to put Jesus Christ on the throne of their life as Lord. "But sanctify the Lord God in your hearts," the Apostle Peter urged (I Peter 3:15). Paul urged essentially the same things of the Romans when he said, "I beseech you therefore, brethren, by the mercies of God, that ye present your bodies a living sacrifice, holy, acceptable unto God, which is your reasonable service" (Romans 12:1). This is the foundation of practicing Biblical stewardship. Stewardship is not just fund raising; it is also managing your life. It is placing your all on the altar for God. Stewardship is recognizing not just the tithe as the Lord's—that is, ten percent—but that all of it is His. "The earth is the Lord's, and the fullness thereof; the world, and they who dwell therein" (Psalm 24:1). He is Lord both by creation and redemption.

Lordship is an experience of the believer rather than the unsaved. What is today referred to as "Lordship Salvation" is almost a statement of salvation by works, but the Scriptures teach that we are saved solely by grace. Lordship is for the Christian; grace is for the unsaved. Failure to recognize Jesus as Lord in your life will result in frustration in your Christian experience. If you never yield control of your life to Jesus, you will constantly have doubts concerning the certainty of your salvation.

Lordship marks the progress or growth of your Christian life

27

as you confess and forsake known sin in the process of becoming more Christlike. George Mueller grew in grace as a Christian. On several occasions God revealed areas in his life to be corrected. As Mueller confessed his sin and surrendered that area of his life to Christ's lordship, he continued to grow in Christ.

Lordship means surrender. In a meeting of several well-known Christian workers in the last century, the question was asked what was the greatest need in Christian circles at that time. Without hesitation, a Scottish missionary leader summed up that need in two words, "absolute surrender." He went on to explain that most of the problems he dealt with in his ministry would resolve themselves if Christians would surrender themselves totally and absolutely to the lordship of Christ. Many Christian leaders today would agree that this is still the greatest need of the church. Jesus said, "If any man will come after me, let him deny himself, and take up his cross daily, and follow me" (Luke 9:23). The key to the victorious Christian life is found in this surrender or yielding of oneself wholeheartedly to God. "Neither yield ye your members as instruments of unrighteousness unto sin: but yield yourselves unto God, as those that are alive from the dead, and your members as instruments of righteousness unto God" (Romans 6:13).

Paul uses four key verbs in Romans 6 which describe various aspects of what it means to call Jesus "Lord." These are keys to the victorious Christian life. The first verb is "know" (6:3,6,9). We must first know the doctrinal basis of victory in the Christian life—that is, that we are united to and identified with Christ in His death and resurrection. The next verb is "reckon" (6:11), which means to count or rely upon these facts to be true concerning ourselves. The verb "yield" (6:13,16,19) means to present ourselves once and for all to God as His possession and for His use. The fourth verb, "obey" (6:16,17), urges us to be continuously obedient to the revealed and known will of God.

Lordship is more than just yielding; lordship means control. An overemphasis on yielding sometimes results in passive Christians. But God wants more than yielded Christians; He wants control of your life. When He has control, we will take up our cross. When He has control, we will deny self and the flesh. When He has control, we will find ourselves saying no to the "old man" and yes to the "new man."

When Jesus taught the parable of the talents, He emphasized several principles of lordship or Biblical stewardship. One of the most significant is that God expects production from what He has given us to use. To take the resources of God, which He has entrusted to our keeping, and hoard them or bury them in the ground is the greatest wrong we can do toward the Lord. When God entrusts us with His resources, He expects us to use them and multiply them. It is impossible to invest what God has given us without seeing a return on it.

CONCLUSION

Recognizing the lordship of Christ should be the norm in the Christian's life. Jesus taught a parable concerning the duty of the servant constantly to obey his master and concluded with the words, "So likewise ye, when ye shall have done all those things which are commanded you, say, We are unprofitable servants: we have done that which was our duty to do" (Luke 17:10). The concept of a Christian who does not recognize the lordship of Christ in his life is foreign to the New Testament ideal.

Yet, such Christians are all too common today. The greatest need of the church is still absolute surrender. Someday, of course, "at the name of Jesus every knee should bow, of things in heaven, and things in earth, and things under the earth: and that every tongue should confess that Jesus Christ is Lord, to the glory of God, the Father" (Philippians 2:10,11). When it

29

comes to recognizing the lordship of Christ, we have a choice. It can be our decision now, or His coercive act later.

For Discussion:

1. What did the word Lord mean in the culture of our Saviour's day?
2. Explain the term "Lordship of Christ."
3. Can you recall a time when you surrendered your life to the Lord? (Be ready to share briefly.)
4. Explain the statement: "Jesus is the Lord of your life whether you let Him operate in your life or not."
5. Where will you be when "everyone" recognizes the Lordship of Christ?

CHAPTER THREE
THE OFFICE OF CHRIST

"Come, see a man, which told me all things that ever I did: is not this the Christ?" (John 4:29).

At least forty-nine times in his Epistles, Paul uses the expression "the/our Lord Jesus Christ," bringing together the three primary names of Jesus. As noted already in our study, "Lord" is His title, "Jesus" is His name, and "Christ" is His office. Actually, "Christ" is a favorite name of the Apostle Paul, and he uses it independently of other titles some 211 times in his writings. In addition, he often uses this title with other names and titles of Christ. For this apostle, the title "Christ" had a very special significance.

The Greek word *Christos,* translated "Christ," literally means "anointed one" and was used in the Septuagint to translate the word "Messiah" (cf. Daniel 9:25,26). The Messiah in the Old Testament and the Christ in the New Testament, therefore, refer to the same Person, although their contextual use affects their perspective somewhat. In the Old Testament, "Messiah" is always used in the context of a Messianic hope, whereas the predominate use of "Christ" in the New Testament is as an official name of Jesus in the context of a work completed.

Theologians speak of the three anointed offices of Christ, meaning Christ as *prophet, priest,* and *king.* This expression seems to have been first used by Eusebius in the third century to explain the Biblical teaching concerning the office of Christ. Even though the writers of Scripture did not express it in so many words, the fact that Christ was viewed by them in the context of the Old Testament anointed offices is particularly evident in the book of Revelation. The title of the book implies the nature of the *prophetic* office in revealing or making known what was otherwise hidden from man (Revelation 1:1). In John's first vision of Christ (1:13), the Lord is viewed wearing a *talar,* a technical word referring to the robe of the *priest.* The office of *king* is seen in Revelation 11:15, where the theme of the book may be summarized: "And the seventh angel sounded; and there were great voices in heaven, saying, The kingdoms of this world are become the kingdoms of our Lord, and of his Christ, and he shall reign forever and ever." This theme is developed throughout the book until the Lord is pictured as returning and having "on his vesture and on his thigh a name written, KING OF KINGS, AND LORD OF LORDS" (19:16).

Although the Old Testament context is important in understanding the implications of the name "Christ," we must again remember that Jesus not only took the reputation of a name upon Himself but also added something of His reputation to the name. This is certainly evident as we see how the Apostle Paul gave the title "Christ" greater clarity in his writings. Paul ministered mostly among Gentiles, to whom the title "Christ" would be meaningless without the Old Testament background. In his various epistles he gave the title "Christ" a fuller meaning for such readers, particularly in the context of the union and communion of Christ and the believer. In many respects, therefore, the apostle must be credited with transforming the office of Christ into a personal name for the One who was the Messiah and much more.

When a young man graduates from medical school and moves to a small town to begin private practice, the members of the community might use the title "Doctor" with great respect as a prefix to his name. But as the years pass and the doctor becomes more and more a part of the community, the title "Doctor" often becomes the nickname "Doc." Similarly, Paul took the title "Messiah" and made it the personal name of Christ by which many Christians today refer to Jesus Christ.

THE MESSIAH IN THE OLD TESTAMENT

Throughout the pages of Old Testament revelation, the prophets of Israel and Judah displayed a pervasive Messianic hope. In their messages, which were often characterized by judgment or doom, often there was also a distant hope that ultimate deliverance would come from God. This deliverance was more than a supernatural phenomenon; it was the work of an anointed servant of God designated "the Messiah" (cf. Daniel 9:25).

This title, which became a name of Jesus, was a title of the preincarnate Christ in that eternal day before the beginning of time. From the very beginning, opposition to God is the same as opposition to "his anointed" (Psalm 2:2). In the consummation of this age, the kingdom of Jehovah is identical to the kingdom "of his Christ" (Revelation 11:15).

In the context of the Old Testament, the term "Messiah" or "Anointed One" had specific relevance to the three offices into which the candidate was normally initiated by an act of anointing—the offices of Prophet, Priest, and King. Because of this I have called it the "Threefold Anointed Office." Prophetically, the coming Messiah ("anointed one") was portrayed as holding each of the offices. Typically, the New Testament identifies Christ in the context of the past principal holders of these offices—namely, the Prophet Moses (cf. Deuteronomy 18:15-19), the Priest Melchizedek (cf. Psalm 110:4), and the King David (II Samuel 7:12,13). The candidate for each of these offices was anointed with oil (cf. I Kings 19:16; Exodus 29:6,7; I Samuel 16:13). In fulfillment of the type, Jesus was anointed by the Holy Spirit as He began His public ministry (Matthew 3:16; Mark 1:10,11; Luke 3:21,22; John 1:32,33).

We must assume that the early disciples understood the title "Christ" in the Old Testament context of "the Messiah." John

33

the Baptist confessed that he, himself, was not the Christ (John 1:20), yet those who left John to follow Jesus announced boldly, "We have found the Messias" (John 1:41). The divine anointing of Jesus for specific service was important in both the teaching of Jesus and the Jerusalem church (cf. Luke 4:18; Acts 10:38). From the very beginning, the early church understood Jesus in terms of His Threefold Anointed Office— Prophet, Priest, and King.

The Anointed Prophet

Few people would deny the prophetic ministry of Jesus even if they might reject the content of His teaching. It is a common practice among those who deny His deity and the unique redemptive nature of His work at least to acknowledge Him to be a moral teacher and religious prophet. Of course, the prophetic office of Christ as revealed in Scripture was far more specific than the vague description of Jesus as a prophet by a liberal teacher.

There are no fewer than five designations which identify the prophet in the Old Testament. First, he was called "the man of God" (Deuteronomy 33:1; I Samuel 2:27; 9:6; I Kings 13:1; Psalm 90:title). This expression related particularly to his unique relationship to God and the uniqueness of his message. Most probably it also assumed that the prophet had a godly character.

The second title of the prophet was the "servant of God" (II Kings 17:13,23; 21:10; 24:2; Ezra 9:11; Jeremiah 7:25). Although no prophet ever called himself the servant of God, God often referred to His prophets as His servants. Some commentators think this might be part of the reason the writers of the New Testament so often began their epistles with such expressions as "servant of God" or "the servant of the Lord Jesus Christ." Also, inasmuch as it was customary for a Jew to begin his prayer to God by identifying himself as the servant of God, we may assume that this title, when applied to the prophets, referred to them as men of prayer. The predominant feature of this designation is that of the Master/slave relationship that existed between God and His servants the prophets.

A third and by far most common designation of the prophet in the Old Testament was the Hebrew word *nabi'*. Although there is some debate as to the origin of this word, scholars generally agree that it derives from an Akkadian root, meaning "to call." The word could be identifying the prophet as one who is called by God, one who calls to men in the name of God, or one who calls to God on behalf of men. In the Old Testament, each of the above descriptions was characteristic of the prophet, and it might be best to think of the term as implying all three aspects.

The final two terms applied to Old Testament prophets derive from Hebrew roots for "sight." *Ro'eh* is an active participle of the verb "to see" and is always translated "seer" in Scripture. The second term, *hozeh,* is an active participle of another verb for "seeing" which has no English equivalent. It is sometimes translated "seer" (I Chronicles 29:29) and sometimes "prophet" (Isaiah 30:10). It is, with one exception, always mentioned in the context of a king, leading some to conclude that this kind of prophet was a resident court historian with prophetic ability (cf. II Chronicles 29:30). First Chronicles 29:29 seems to prove that these three Hebrew terms distinguish three varieties within the prophetic office, for the verse uses each term of different persons who were prophets. That there are similarities in these three kinds of prophets is evidenced in passages such as Amos 7:12ff., where Amaziah addresses Amos as a *hozel,* asking him to prophesy *(nabi')* in Judah. Amos on that occasion refused, claiming he was not a *nabi'*.

In the New Testament, two Greek verbs identify prophesying. The word *prophaino* means "to reveal" and includes the idea of predicting the future and revealing the message of God.

35

The other term, *prothemi,* conveys the meaning "to tell forth," to speak to others on behalf of God though not necessarily with a predictive message. The noun *prophetes* was used by the Greeks as early as the fourth century B.C. to identify those who could interpret the oracles of the gods. The word literally refers to one who speaks forth or openly, and was loosely applied to anyone who proclaimed a divine message. The word *prophetes* was used in the Old Testament Greek version (the Septuagint or LXX) to translate both *nabi'* and *ro'eh*. It, therefore, came to be understood by the Jews to refer to one anointed of the Holy Spirit who received revelation from and communicated a message for God.

One of the early Messianic prophecies of the Old Testament was that God would raise up a Prophet like unto Moses (Deuteronomy 18:15). Although the character of this Prophet came to be the standard by which other prophets were evaluated, the Jews clearly understood the prophecy as Messianic. Many Old Testament prophets engaged in prophecy, but only Jesus possessed the credentials and practiced the ministry of the Prophet in perfection. His ministry gave evidence of all three of the following aspects of prophetic preaching:

Spokesman for God—"For-teller" Jesus was a spokesman for God and so fulfilled the office of the prophet. Everything Jesus said was the Word of God. Also, "His name is called the Word of God" (Revelation 19:13). Jesus consciously said and did the will of the Father while here on earth. He told the religious leaders of His day, "The Son can do nothing of himself, but what he seeth the Father do: for what things soever he doeth, these also doeth the Son likewise" (John 5:19). Later in the same conversation, Jesus said, "I can of mine own self do nothing: as I hear, I judge: and my judgment is just; because I seek not mine own will, but the will of the Father who hath sent me" (John 5:30).

Prediction—"Foreteller" Normally, when people think of

prophecy, their first idea is that of predicting future events. In His role as foreteller, Jesus made several prophecies. He told His disciples about the coming of the Holy Spirit (John 14:26), which was fulfilled at Pentecost (Acts 2:1-4). Further, He described the ministry of the Holy Spirit in this age (John 16:13,14) and the details of His own death, burial, and resurrection (Matthew 16:21). Additional predictive teachings of Christ dealt with His return (John 14:2,3), the existence of the church (Matthew 16:18), and the course of the church age (Matthew 13).

A Preacher to People—"Forth-teller" Jesus taught the people truth concerning God. Nicodemus, a Pharisee and ruler of the Jews, acknowledged, "Rabbi, we know that thou art a teacher come from God: for no man can do these miracles that thou doest, except God be with him" (John 3:2). When Jesus taught, "the people were astonished at his doctrine; for he taught them as one having authority" (Matthew 7:28,29). Jesus spoke with authority for God. Several extended discourses of Jesus are recorded in Scripture, including the Sermon on the Mount (Matthew 5—7), the mystery parables (Matthew 13), the Olivet discourse (Matthew 24—25), and the Upper Room discourse (John 13—16).

Jesus was certainly consistent with the prophetic tradition of Israel; and, as such, those who heard Him understood Him to be a prophet (cf. Matthew 14). But Jesus was more than just another prophet; He was *the* Prophet. Although there were many similarities between Jesus and the other prophets, there were also differences. The most notable of these was His authority in preaching. The prophet of God almost always prefaced his remarks with the expression "Thus saith the Lord"; but, characteristically, Jesus began by saying, "But I say unto you."

The Anointed Priest

A second anointed office in the Old Testament was that of

the priest. Primarily, the priest acted as man's representative before God. The priest offered the sacrifice upon the altar. Because God is by nature both just and forgiving, the priest could always tell the people God would forgive them if they met His conditions. The priest was a channel of forgiveness, whereas the prophet was usually the channel of judgment. Priests were, by far, more popular than prophets.

The office of the priest was an anointed office because the candidate could not practice this office until he was first dipped in water and anointed with oil. This normally occurred at age thirty, and for twenty years the candidate then served as a functioning priest. It is significant that Luke notes this was the age of Jesus when He was baptized by John and anointed with the Holy Spirit (cf. Luke 3:23).

The fullest development of New Testament teaching on the priesthood of Christ is understandably in the book of Hebrews. There it is demonstrated that He is both a priest and a high priest. His priesthood is considered superior because it succeeds to the order of Melchizedek rather than of Aaron. Some commentators have interpreted this claim to mean that Melchizedek was a Christophany, but it is more likely we should view him as a type of Christ! Actually, "Melchizedek" was not a name but a dynastic title, which may also be applied to Jesus. This explains why the Scriptures appear to call Melchizedek "Jesus." In reality, they are calling Jesus "Melchizedek."

The office of the priest was unique in nature. First, if one was a priest, the implication is that he had been called of God to that task. Also, as a priest, he could represent another before God. If Jesus is a priest, then He serves two major functions—that of offering sacrifices and that of intercession for others.

Jesus was not only a priest but also the High Priest. In addition to his other responsibilities as a priest, the High Priest was particularly involved in the activities of the Day of Atonement

(Leviticus 16) and in the use of the Urim and Thummin (Numbers 27:21). He was Israel's mediator on the Day of Atonement, for he took the blood of the slaughtered goat into the Holy of holies, where he offered propitiation for the nation's sins and effected the atonement or covering of their sin for another year. He wore the Urim and Thummin on his breastplate, which contained the names of the twelve tribes and, as such, represented the nation. By using this means, he alone could discern the will of God for the nation. In contrast with the limited national ministry of Israel's High Priest, Jesus "is the propitiation for our sins: and not for ours only, but also for the sins of the whole world" (I John 2:2).

The names "priest" and "High Priest" primarily relate to the redemptive work of Christ, for they help explain it within the context of the legal system of Moses. Yet, these names also relate to His person as He fulfilled the ideal qualifications for these offices. He is in both person and ministry our *priest, high priest, propitiation, mediator,* and *guide.* Many of the secondary names of Jesus to some extent belong to the function and office of the priest.

The Anointed King

In the Old Testament one of the designations of the coming Messiah was that of Israel's king (cf. Psalm 2:7; Zechariah 9:9). It is interesting to note Nathanael's recognition of Jesus as "the Son of God . . . the King of Israel" (John 1:49). In the Gospel of Mark, the title "King" occurs six times but always as a term of contempt or derision. It is the Gospel of Matthew that really develops this theme. Matthew begins with the legal genealogy of Jesus, noting Him to be the legal heir to the throne of David. The number fourteen is particularly emphasized in this genealogy (cf. Matthew 1:17). This is significant for two reasons. First, the numerical value of the name "David" is fourteen. Secondly, fourteen is the product of two times seven,

seven being the number of perfection or completeness. Most Jews considered David their most nearly perfect king, and Matthew is introducing the "second David." Although several kings are listed in the genealogy, only David is called king.

In the next chapter of Matthew, the magi looking for Jesus ask, "Where is he that is born King of the Jews?" (2:2); and Herod responds by inquiring of the chief priests and scribes "where Christ should be born" (2:4). Matthew develops this theme further until he records Jesus Himself acknowledging, "All power is given unto me in heaven and in earth" (28:18). Jesus is the king with ultimate authority.

When the early church practiced the implications of this aspect of who Christ is, it was not without negative consequences. They called Jesus their king (Acts 17:7), recognizing Him alone as the supreme Ruler in their lives; but this was offensive to Rome, who viewed Caesar as both god and king. Much of the later persecution of the church was related to Rome's view that recognition of Jesus as king was seditious. It is, therefore, significant that the theme of the final book written to the persecuted church is the regal status of Jesus (cf. Revelation 11:15; 19:16).

Jesus is King   The kingship of Christ follows from His deity. Because He is God, He is also king. Paul gave praise to King Jesus: "Unto the King eternal, immortal, invisible, the only wise God, be honor and glory forever and ever" (I Timothy 1:17). In heaven "they sing the song of Moses the servant of God, and the song of the Lamb, saying, Great and marvelous are thy works, Lord God Almighty; just and true are thy ways, thou King of saints" (Revelation 15:3). The Romans considered their Caesar to be a god. Christians, on the other hand, recognized Jesus alone to be their king. Calling Jesus "king" implied they believed in His deity.

Jesus has a kingdom   Every king has a domain over which he rules, and Jesus is no exception. He acknowledged, "My kingdom is not of this world" (John 18:36), but He never denied He had a kingdom. It was the custom of the Romans to identify the crime of a condemned man by writing it on a shingle and nailing it on the cross upon which he died. Jesus was executed as "the King of the Jews" (John 19:19). When He returns to this earth, He will do so to establish His kingdom for a thousand years (Revelation 20:1-6).

Jesus has subjects   Christ is now a ruler to those who submit their wills to Him. Someday, "at the name of Jesus every knee should bow, of things in heaven, and things in earth and things under the earth, and . . . every tongue should confess that Jesus is Lord" (Philippians 2:10,11). Today, those who receive Christ as Lord and Saviour recognize the kingship of Christ in their lives. Jesus taught a parable which equated His disciples with servants (Luke 17:10), and that was the attitude of the early church. They were eager to serve their King.

THE CHRIST IN THE NEW TESTAMENT

Many of the New Testament references to Christ must be understood in the context of the Old Testament Messiah. This is the probable meaning when Peter confessed Jesus was "the Christ, the Son of the living God" (Matthew 16:16), and when Caiaphas asked Jesus whether He was the Christ (Matthew 26:63). On the day of Pentecost, Peter concluded his sermon by declaring Jesus to be "both Lord and Christ" (Acts 2:36), again to be understood in the context of the Old Testament Messiah. But "Christ" was also the favorite title of Paul, who ministered primarily among Gentiles that lacked the understanding of the Jews concerning the Messiah. In Paul's letters the title "Christ" took on a special significance—a new dimension.

Jesus did not use the title directly of Himself, although He answered "I am" when people asked Him whether He was the Christ (Mark 14:62), and He approved of others calling Him by that title (John 4:25,26; Matthew 16:16,17). On occasion He also mentioned that His disciples belonged to Christ, although we cannot be conclusive from the context that He was necessarily referring to Himself (Mark 9:41; Matthew 23:10).

In his epistles, Paul often used the title "Christ" with the name "Jesus," and when he did so, the order of the names was significant. The name "Christ Jesus" referred to the exalted One who emptied Himself (Philippians 2:5-9), emphasizing His preexistence and having reference to His grace. The reverse order of "Jesus Christ," however, referred to the despised and rejected One who was afterward glorified (Philippians 2:11).

One of the great themes in Paul's epistles was that of the union and communion of the believer with Christ. In this connection, he uses the expression "in Christ" 172 times and speaks also of Christ's indwelling the believer. Interestingly enough, it is always "Christ," never "Jesus," that he uses to teach indwelling. Paul's use of this title of Jesus is foundational to our understanding of the Christian life.

Union with Christ—Our Position in Heaven

The expression "in Christ" refers to our union with Christ, an aspect of the Christian's experience of salvation. Being "in Christ" is a non-experiential state—that is, it occurs at the moment of salvation in the life of every believer, whether he realizes it or not. This is our position or standing in Heaven. In Paul's writings "Christ" becomes the positional name of Jesus after His resurrection.

The nature of the union between Christ and the believer is difficult to define and may be best understood if we describe several aspects of this relationship. Although in themselves each aspect falls short of what this union is, together they give us a more complete portrait of the nature of this union.

This union is a mystical union, for, in a sense, there is a blending of the life of God into the life of the believer so that, although believers remain distinct persons, there is the development of oneness in will and purpose. This union transcends the limits even of the marriage union. By this union we also become Jesus' friend (cf. John 15:14,15).

Secondly, there is a legal or federal aspect of this union. In this sense, our union with Christ becomes the basis of our justification and adoption. It is legal or federal in the sense that we are in our lawyer or senator while he represents us before the court or in government. Again, although this is one aspect of our union, it also goes much deeper.

Our union is of an organic nature in which not only does the believer become a member of the body of Christ, but Christ also becomes a part of the believer. Furthermore the Christian life is the result of a vital union with Christ. It is Christ living in us, not merely influencing us from without. Because the Holy Spirit is the author of this union, we call it a spiritual union.

Moreover, this union is both indissoluble and inscrutable. The believer is so bonded to Christ that he has entered into an indissoluble relationship with Him. The omnipresence of Christ makes this union possible. Also, because this union involves the nature of God, there is a sense in which we can never fully understand it.

Finally, the union of the believer and Christ must be regarded as both complete and completed. To speak of a believer partially united with Christ is as impossible as to speak of a woman who is only partially pregnant. Although we may grow in the realization of this truth, we are never more deeply united with Christ by any means than we are at conversion.

Communion with Christ—Our Experience on Earth

Not only are we "in Christ," but Christ is also in us. This is the basis of our communion with Christ, which is an experience of our sanctification. The writings of Paul sometimes use the title "Christ" without the article. Paul does this consistently in order to signify the One who by the Holy Spirit and also His own Person indwells the believer and molds the believer's character into a closer conformity to Christ (Romans

43

8:10; Galatians 2:20; 4:19; Ephesians 3:17). The practical application of this truth results in our abiding in Christ.

Many writers distinguish two aspects of abiding in Christ. First, it means to have no known sin unjudged and unconfessed so as to hinder our communion or fellowship with Christ. Secondly, it assumes that we give all burdens and concerns to Him and rely upon Him for the strength, wisdom, faith, and character we need to meet the particular challenges of life. Not only is His position our position (union), but His life is also our life (communion).

CONCLUSION

When the prophets of Israel and Judah spoke of the coming Messiah, their highest thoughts of Him were those of Prophet, Priest, and King. Jesus functions today in each of those offices in the life of the believer. But He is also far more. He is no longer merely "the Christ" but also "Christ," the One in whom we dwell and depend upon for the very essence of spiritual life and the One who lives within, providing all that is necessary for effective Christian living.

For Discussion:

1. What is the literal meaning of the name Christ? Why was it Paul's favorite name for the Saviour?
2. How did Christ fulfill His office as prophet?
3. As an anointed priest, how does Christ minister to us today?
4. Describe the kingdom and rule of Jesus Christ, the King.
5. God's Word teaches that believers are "in Christ" and Christ abides in believers. What effect does this have on your everyday life?

PART TWO

Groupings of the Names of Jesus Christ

CHAPTER FOUR
THE OLD TESTAMENT PROPHETIC NAMES OF JESUS

"Philip findeth Nathanael, and saith unto him, We have found him, of whom Moses in the law, and the prophets, did write, Jesus of Nazareth, the son of Joseph" (John 1:45).

"And beginning at Moses and all the prophets, he expounded unto them, in all the scriptures the things concerning himself" (Luke 24:27).

It often has been said that the Old Testament is Christ concealed and the New Testament is Christ revealed, and yet, the Old Testament was the Bible by which the early church preached the gospel of Christ to a lost world. Hidden in the pages of law, history, poetry, and prophecy is a wealth of revelation concerning the Lord Jesus Christ. He is revealed in every book through types, metaphors, analogies, and indisputable titles. Although it would be impossible for us to consider every title in a single chapter, we shall discuss in this chapter several of the principal titles of Jesus Christ in the Old Testament. Some important Old Testament names are omitted here because they are covered in later chapters.

SHILOH

One of the earliest of the titles the book of Genesis applies to the coming Messiah in the Old Testament is "Shiloh." As Jacob was blessing his sons and prophesying concerning the twelve tribes of Israel, he said: "The sceptre shall not depart from Judah, nor a lawgiver from between his feet, until Shiloh come; and unto him shall the gathering of the people be" (Genesis 49:10).

46

The name *Shiloh* means "peace maker" and closely relates to one of Isaiah's birth names for Jesus, "the Prince of Peace" (Isaiah 9:6). This prophecy affirms that Shiloh would come from the royal tribe of Judah, wield a temporal scepter, and possess a sovereignty of a different character.

PROPHET

The great prophet in the history of Israel was Moses, although before he died, he prophesied of a future Prophet that the Jews came to understand to be the coming Messiah. "The Lord thy God will raise up unto thee a Prophet from the midst of thee, of thy brethren, like unto me; unto him ye shall hearken" (Deuteronomy 18:15). This prophet would speak as a forthteller, preaching a message; as a for-teller, preaching for God; and as a fore-teller, predicting things to come. The preaching of Jesus conformed to each aspect of this prophetic preaching.

THE BRANCH

Our English Bible translates three Hebrew words "branch" as a name or title of Jesus. The first word, *tsemach,* literally refers to a green shoot or sprout growing out of an old stump. A similar word, *netser,* was used of a small, fresh green twig. A third word, translated "rod" in Isaiah 11:1, was *choter;* this refers to a shoot growing out of a cut-down stump. These three words describe Jesus as "the Branch."

This title of Christ had both positive and negative connotations. A puzzling verse in Matthew refers to an Old Testament prophecy to the effect, "He shall be called a Nazarene" (Matthew 2:23). To be called a Nazarene by those living outside Nazareth was insulting, for the town had a reputation as the city of garbage. Even one of Jesus' first disciples asked, "Can any good thing come out of Nazareth?" (John 1:46). But the puzzling thing about this verse is that no verse in the Old Testament identifies Nazareth as the home of the Messiah. Most commentators argue that Matthew was here alluding to one of the Branch prophecies, having noted the similarity of sound between *netser* and Nazareth.

Isaiah did use the word *netzer* in a negative sense when he said of the king of Babylon, "But thou art cast out of thy grave like an abominable branch" (Isaiah 14:19). Here the word describes a useless shoot cut off a tree and left to rot. Although Isaiah's use of the word in this context does not specifically refer to Christ, it does demonstrate how Matthew could have understood a Branch prophecy to imply that Jesus would have to live with the reputation of being a Nazarene.

Positively, these words for "Branch" are used in four ways corresponding to the four Gospels in the New Testament. First, Christ is the King Branch. This corresponds to the Gospel of Matthew, which emphasizes the life of Christ as the King of the Jews. Jeremiah noted, "Behold, the days come, saith the Lord, that I will raise unto David a righteous Branch, and a King shall reign and prosper, and shall execute judgment and justice in the earth" (Jeremiah 23:5). This title specifically applies to the coming kingdom of God during the millennial reign of Christ.

Jesus is also spoken of as a Servant Branch. This corresponds to the Gospel of Mark, which portrays Jesus as the Servant of the Lord. The prophet Zechariah announced, "Hear now, O Joshua the high priest, thou, and thy fellows that sit before thee: for they are men wondered at: for, behold, I will bring forth my servant, the BRANCH" (Zechariah 3:8). Jesus was not only a king but a servant. Several passages in Isaiah more fully describe this One who is the Servant of Jehovah.

This Branch is described as a man. This corresponds to the unique emphasis of the Gospel of Luke, which eighty times refers to Jesus as the Son of man. Again, it was the prophet Zechariah who announced this aspect of the Branch. "And speak unto him, saying, Thus speaketh the Lord of hosts, saying,

Behold the man whose name is The BRANCH; and he shall grow up out of his place, and he shall build the temple of the Lord'' (Zechariah 6:12).

The final aspect of the Branch is that the Lord Himself is the Branch. This corresponds to the emphasis of the Gospel of John, which begins with a statement as to the deity of Jesus the Word. ''In that day shall the branch of the Lord be beautiful and glorious, and the fruit of the earth shall be excellent and comely for those who are escaped of Israel'' (Isaiah 4:2). Again, this name specifically applies to the millennial reign of Christ still to come.

THE DESIRE OF ALL NATIONS

Perhaps no preacher in history left behind such a brief record of ministry with as great accomplishment as the prophet Haggai. The book which records his name consists of five sermons that range in length from a single line to several verses. Yet, it was primarily the preaching of this prophet that led to the resumption of work and completion of the second temple in Jerusalem. Because some Jews had seen the previous temple in all its physical splendor, they became discouraged as they saw the builders erecting a smaller wood frame structure. Haggai knew the people were failing to realize it was not the architecture of a building but rather God's presence that made a building a holy place. To encourage the people, Haggai prophesied of the days when ''the desire of all nations shall come'' (Haggai 2:7).

Commentators debate among themselves about the meaning of this phrase ''desire of all nations.'' Some argue Haggai meant the wealth of other nations—that is, the desirable things of those nations—would someday be brought to this second temple. A more probable interpretation is that the phrase is a title of Christ, who would come to the temple that seemed so insignificant in the eyes of some of the workers.

49

Jewish writers have noted that the second temple lacked five objects which were present in the first temple: the ark of the covenant with its mercy seat or place of propitiation, the tables of the law, the holy fire, the sacred oracle in the breastplate of the high priest, and the Shekinah glory of God. Although God did not give these things to the remnant that returned and built the temple, He did promise to send the "desire of all nations" who was all these things and more.

Jesus is the reality of which the ark was only the type. He is not only the place of propitiation but "the propitiation for our sins" (I John 2:2). The early Christians applied the title "Lawgiver" to the Lord (James 4:12). He is a "wall of fire," the "Urim and Thummin," and our "High Priest." But above all these things, He is the incarnate "Shekinah glory of God." As the Apostle John noted, "And the Word was made flesh, and dwelt among us (and we beheld his glory, the glory as of the only begotten of the Father), full of grace and truth" (John 1:14). The Shekinah glory was indeed absent at the dedication of the second temple, but eventually it was present in Christ in a greater sense than ever was true of the first temple. The "desire of all nations" has come; He was the fullness of the Godhead, and He dwelt or tabernacled among us.

Although this prophecy had partial fulfillment in the first advent of Christ, many commentators point out that the context of this prophecy applies to the second coming of Christ. In the millennium Christ will be King and Lord of the nations. In that sense, the "desire of all nations" is still yet to come. However, in a sense He is the "desirable one of all nations" today, since Christians around the world echo the final prayer of the Scriptures, "Even so, come, Lord Jesus" (Revelation 22:20).

THE ENSIGN OF THE PEOPLES

One of the many titles for Christ in the book of Isaiah is "an ensign of the peoples" (Isaiah 11:10). Of the seven times the word "ensign" appears in Scripture, six are singular and found in the prophecy of Isaiah. The word itself refers to a national flag to which people rally. It is the symbol of the nation, and loyalty to that flag is the most common form of patriotism.

While I served as President of Winnipeg Bible College, the Canadian government redesigned a new national flag. At the time a great debate arose over the proposed action. Many Canadians remembered fighting for liberty in World War II and the Korean War under the old Red Ensign. To change that flag seemed unpatriotic and an attack on the national heritage of Canadians. Today, almost two decades later, most Canadians feel a sense of deep-seated patriotism when they see their new Maple Leaf flag blowing in the wind. Just as the old Red Ensign was an untouchable symbol of the nation in the early sixties, so many Canadians would respond the same way if the government tried to change the flag today and abandon the Maple Leaf flag.

In the same way in which a nation rallies around its flag, Christians rally around Jesus. The history of the church is a record of various conflicts and debates over different interpretations of doctrine, but true Christianity has always been grounded upon an agreement concerning Christ. There were times when good men thought it wrong to baptize, wrong to send out missionaries, or wrong to be involved in political action, but they have always found a rallying point around the person and work of Jesus Christ. He has been the Ensign to which they have been drawn.

As "an ensign for the peoples," Jesus is not just the flag which brings a group of Christians from one country together but, rather, the flag which brings believers from all places together. Commenting on this title of Christ, Charles J. Rolls exclaimed,

> What a distinction! To be high above all principality and power.

51

What a recognition! To be revered by myriad hosts of men and angels.
What a coronation! To be crowned Lord of lords and King of kings.
What a commemoration! To be admired in all them that believe.

EL SHADDAI — THE ALMIGHTY

When the Lord appeared to Abraham to confirm His covenant with him, He revealed Himself to the ninety-nine-year-old man of faith as *El Shaddai* (Genesis 17:1). Linguists do not agree about the etymology of this title and usually suggest one of three possibilities. Some link the word to the Hebrew *shadad*, meaning "to devastate," and argue the title lays emphasis on the irresistible power of God. Others believe the word relates the Akkadian word *shadu*, meaning "mountain," and argue the title means something like "God of the Mountains." The third and most probable meaning of this word is based on its relationship to the Hebrew word *shad*, meaning "breast."

El Shaddai is naturally a tender title for God. Scripture uses it exclusively of God in relation to His children. When trying to explain more fully the implications of this name, some writers have spoken of "the mother-love of God." To the child held to his mother's breast, the mother is the all-sufficient one who provides both the physical necessities and emotional support the child needs. Similarly *El Shaddai* is the all-sufficient One in the believer's experience. He has been accurately described as "the God who is enough."

El Shaddai was Job's favorite name for God. Thirty-one of its forty-eight occurrences in Scripture appear in the book of Job. For Job in the midst of his suffering and despair, *El Shaddai* was enough. This title suggests supplying the need and comforting the hurt. Over the years, many Christians have discovered the true nature of *El Shaddai* only in their darkest hours. When we understand this name of Jesus, we can grow in our Christian experience, knowing the tenderness that characterizes Christ, until we can confess with Job, "Though he slay me, yet will I trust in him" (Job 13:15).

CONCLUSION

Throughout the Old Testament the prophets of God looked forward to the day when their coming Messiah would arrive. As God continued to reveal more and more about Him, they chose names to describe Him more accurately. Hundreds of such names appear in the pages of the Old Testament but they describe only part of the character and nature of Jesus. Although these names were given to nourish a sense of anticipation and expectation, we can enjoy them even more, for now at least in part the fulfillment has come. Jesus has proved to be far more than what the prophets could have imagined.

For Discussion:

1. What is probably the earliest name of Christ in the Old Testament? What do we know about our Saviour from this title?
2. One of the favorite titles for Christ in the prophets was Branch. How is Christ our Branch?
3. Haggai called Christ "the desire of all nations." How does Christ fulfill this title?
4. Isaiah called Christ "the ensign of the people." What should be our reaction to this name?
5. Share an experience when you realized that Christ is your El Shaddai.

CHAPTER FIVE
THE SALVATIONAL NAMES OF JESUS

"For I know that my redeemer liveth, and that he shall stand at the latter day upon the earth" (Job 19:25).

"Let the words of my mouth, and the meditation of my heart, be acceptable in thy sight, O LORD, my strength, and my redeemer" (Psalm 19:14).

Theologians refer to certain names and titles of Jesus Christ as the soteriological titles because they have particular reference to the work of Christ in salvation. I call these names the "salvational names of Jesus" because they are the names which reveal or clarify our salvation more fully. Although the Bible speaks of salvation in three tenses (past, present and future), the names I'll discuss in this chapter refer primarily to salvation past— that is, to our conversion rather than our sanctification and eventual glorification with Christ. We might designate these names as evangelistic names, for they tend to preach or explain the *evangel* or gospel of salvation.

REDEEMER

When we think of the doctrine of salvation, sooner or later we must consider the concept of redemption. It is a little surprising, however, that the title "Redeemer" is never used of Jesus in the New Testament although its verbal form occurs both in the Gospels and Epistles in connection with His work of redemption (Luke 1:68; 24:21; Galatians 3:13; 4:5; Titus 2:14; I Peter 1:18; Revelation 5:9; 14:3,4). This name was, nevertheless, a popular title in the Old Testament, particularly in the Psalms (Job 19:25; Psalm 19:14).

54

Although the New Testament does not call Jesus "Redeemer," it certainly emphasizes His work of redemption throughout. The term "redemption" comes from a word which means "to buy back." Christ gave His blood as a ransom for sin; by it He redeems the lost (I Peter 1:18-20). In the context of soteriology, the price of redemption is blood which is paid to procure the remission of sins (Hebrews 9:12,22). The Greek words for "redeemed" denote the purchase of servants in the ancient slave market. The Bible applies the terms to the redemption of all men.

First, the Bible teaches that Christ purchased the sinner in the marketplace. The verb *agorazo* means "to go to the marketplace *(agora)* and pay the price for a slave." The verb was common in deeds of sale and generally meant the paying of a price for a group of slaves. Those who were "sold under sin" are redeemed (Galatians 3:10). Each of the following Scriptures uses the term *agorazo:* Revelation 14:3,4 speaks of the 144,000 as those redeemed from the earth; Revelation 5:9 notes that Christ's blood was the price paid for redemption; and II Peter 2:1 shows that Christ redeemed (paid the price) not only for the saved but also for the false teachers. *Agorazo* is simply the payment, the purchase price—the price of redemption, which is blood.

A second word in the Bible for "redemption" is *ekagorazo,* meaning "to buy out from the marketplace." The prefix *ek* means "out." Therefore, this term refers to the fact that Christ paid the price with His blood and bought the slave "out of the marketplace" of sin. The slave was never again exposed to sale (Galatians 3:13). When Christ took man out from under the Law, He placed him in a different relationship with God by providing for him the opportunity to become an adopted son of God (Galatians 4:5). *Ekagorazo* emphasizes the removal of the curse of the Law (Galatians 3:13; 4:5).

The third word which refers to redemption is *lutrao.* This

55

word means "to pay the price for the slave and then release him" (Galatians 4:5). It emphasizes the freedom that Christ brings to those whom He redeemed. This verb suggests that Christ works to separate us completely from all sin (Titus 2:14).

A consideration of each of these terms and the contexts in which they appear in the New Testament indicates Christ has provided redemption for all people by the shedding of His own blood (Hebrews 9:12). That redemption includes the price of redemption *(agorazo)*, removal from the marketplace of sin *(ekagorazo)*, and the provision of liberty to the redeemed *(lutrao)*. This is the work of the Redeemer. But the sinner is not prepared to go to Heaven until he responds by faith to the Redeemer.

SAVIOUR

It is interesting that Scripture rarely uses the name "Saviour" of Jesus, especially in view of the fact that "Saviour" is fundamental to all Jesus is and did. At His birth the angel announced, "For unto you is born this day in the city of David a Saviour, which is Christ the Lord" (Luke 2:11). Early in His ministry, a group of Samaritans concluded the same truth and told the woman who met Jesus at Sychar's well, "Now we believe, not because of thy saying: for we have heard him ourselves, and know that this is indeed the Christ, the Saviour of the world" (John 4:42). But these are the only two instances in the Gospels of this title being applied to Jesus. He is seldom called "Saviour" in the Epistles although both Peter (Acts 5:31) and Paul (Acts 13:23) used this title of Christ in their preaching.

Men have wondered why this name that embodies the very essence of the work of Christ should be almost neglected by the apostles. Two reasons suggest themselves. First, the apostles may have been trying to avoid a major confrontation with Roman authorities. One of the titles of Caesar was "Saviour of the World." A second reason for its infrequent use may have been that all Christ is and does in His saving work led the New Testament writers to take the title for granted. Both Peter and Paul used this title in an evangelistic appeal where they were trying to explain the fundamentals of the gospel. If this were characteristic of the evangelical preaching of the early church, we would not expect a special emphasis in epistles, which were written largely to correct problems in the church. The emphasis on Jesus as Saviour may be absent because early believers widely understood and accepted it.

The Greek word *soter* means "a saviour," "deliverer" or "preserver." It is a title used of the Father as well as the Son. It shares a common root with the verb *sozo,* which is the most commonly used expression of conversion in the Scriptures. This verb is used in three tenses in the New Testament to describe complete and full salvation. First, the believer has been saved from the guilt and penalty of sin. Secondly, he is being saved from the habit and dominion of sin. Thirdly, he will be saved at the return of Christ from all the bodily infirmities and curse that result from sin.

THE LAMB OF GOD

In the first twenty-six books of the New Testament only John the Baptist uses the title "Lamb of God." The expression occurs twenty-six times in the final book of the New Testament. When we think of the book of Revelation, we usually think of the Lord as "the Lion of the Tribe of Judah"—that is, the coming king, but the most frequent title of Christ in that book is "the Lamb." The reason is that His coming as king is possible only because of His sacrifice as a lamb.

Being the son of a priest, John the Baptist was no doubt familiar with the importance of the lamb offered every morning and evening in a whole burnt offering. He was acquainted as well with the other sacrifices, including Passover. This title of Christ probably derived from Isaiah's description of the "Suffering Servant of the Lord" (Isaiah 53) and the levitical system of sacrifice in Israel. Just as a lamb was offered on the altar for sin, so the Lamb of God would be offered for the sin of the world.

John predicted that the Lamb of God would take away sin. The verb *airon,* translated "taketh away," conveys the idea of taking something up and carrying it away and, in that sense, destroying it. Jesus took away sin by bearing it in His own body (I Peter 2:24), and so, He removed our transgressions from us as far as the east is from the west (Psalm 103:12). Even before the cross John spoke of Jesus as the Lamb already taking away sin.

At least ten times Scripture speaks about the taking away of sin:

WHEN THE LAMB OF GOD TAKES AWAY SIN

1. Before the foundation of the world (Revelation 13:8)
2. At the Fall of man (Genesis 3:15)
3. With the offering of a sacrifice (Genesis 4:7)
4. On the Day of Atonement (Leviticus 16:34)
5. At a time of national repentance (II Chronicles 7:14)
6. During the public ministry of Jesus (John 1:29)
7. On the cross (I Peter 2:24)
8. At conversion (Romans 6:6)
9. At the Second Coming (Romans 8:18-23)
10. At the end of the millennium (Revelation 20:15; 21:8)

PROPITIATION

A title of Christ which relates to the Lamb of God is "The Propitiation." The Greek word *hilaskomai* occurred in pagan literature to describe the sacrifices offered to idols in order to appease their wrath. The translators of the Septuagint used this word in a technical sense to identify the mercy seat, the place of reconciliation between God and man. The term conveys the idea of a full satisfaction to appease the wrath of God. Jesus bore the full brunt of God's wrath, and so He is the Propitiation for sin (I John 2:2).

In an effort to escape the connotation that the wrath of God must be appeased, some translators prefer to translate this term "expiation." They consider "propitiation" applies in Scripture only to pagan deities. But this view fails to recognize the offensiveness of sin in the eyes of God and the reality of the wrath of God against sin.

That Jesus is our Propitiation has deep meaning for every believer. First it is the basis of our salvation. The so-called "sinner's prayer," "God be merciful to me a sinner" (Luke 18:13), is literally, "God be propitious to me the sinner." Also, it is the incentive for our love for other Christians. "Herein is love, not that we loved God, but that he loved us, and sent his Son to be the propitiation for our sins. Beloved, if God so loved us, we ought also to love one another" (I John 4:10,11).

THE LAST ADAM

The Apostle Paul taught that the human race consisted of two groups—those who were "in Adam" and those who were "in Christ." In presenting this contrast, he used several comparative names of Christ, including "the Last Adam" (I Corinthians 15:45) and "the Second Man" (I Corinthians 15:47). These two related titles are fundamental to the doctrine of imputation, the means by which God reckons our sin to Christ and His righteousness to us.

When we speak of "the headship of the race," we do so in two senses. First, Adam was the Federal Head of the race and when he sinned, we sinned in the same sense that when our representative government takes a course of action, we who elected certain candidates as our leaders are also involved in the decisions they make. Secondly, Adam was the Seminal Head of the race in that he was the physical father of the human race. When Adam sinned, he became a sinner by nature, a nature

59

which we as Adam's descendants also received, much as the child of a mother who is a drug addict may be born with an addiction to that drug.

Christ as the Last Adam and Second Man is the head of a new race in the same way Adam was the head of the old race. When He died for us, He paid the price for our sin on our behalf much as a government might pay off its national debt, which is the debt also of those who elected that government. When Christ rose from the dead, He did so as a quickening or life-giving spirit, able and willing to impart new life to all who come to Him.

History and society are the result of two men and their respective acts. Adam, by disobedience, plunged this world into the slavery of sin. Jesus, by obedience, brought this world back to Himself. Because of what the first Adam did, we need to be saved. Because of what the Last Adam did, we may be saved. In order to be saved, we must be "in" the Last Adam.

AUTHOR OF ETERNAL SALVATION

Describing Jesus, the writer to the Hebrews notes, "He became the author of eternal salvation unto all them that obey him" (Hebrews 5:9). The Greek word used here for salvation is *aitios,* which denotes that which causes something else. He is the "Author of Salvation" as one might be an author of a novel. The author knows all that is to be written before the book is published. He develops the plan of the book, its underlying thesis, the characters, and plot or story line. And when the book is completed, it contains a part of the author, an investment of a part of his life.

When we speak of Jesus as "the Author of Eternal Salvation," this illustration is accurate only in part. Jesus is not merely the formal cause of salvation, He is the efficacious and active cause of it. Not only is salvation caused or effected by Christ, but He is Salvation itself (Luke 2:30; 3:6). Although an author may invest a part of himself in his book, we cannot say the book is the author. But Jesus is that of which He is the author. When the Scriptures reveal Him as the "Author of Eternal Salvation," it emphasizes not only His ability to save but also His power to keep.

Closely related to this title of Christ are several titles which make use of the Greek word *archegos,* translated in Scripture as "prince," "author," and "captain." This is the key word in the titles "Prince of life" (Acts 3:15), "a Prince and a Saviour" (Acts 5:31), "the captain of their salvation" (Hebrews 2:10), and "the author and finisher of our faith" (Hebrews 12:2). The term signifies one who takes the lead in something or provides the first occasion of anything. In his English translation of the Scriptures, Moffat consistently translates this word "pioneer." Although translated "author" once in the New Testament, the word really stresses quality of leadership; it does not necessarily mean that the cause originated with the leader. This is, of course, true of Christ as noted in the above title but not implied in the use of this related Greek word. The emphasis here is that of His primacy. As the *aitios,* He originates and provides eternal salvation for all who will come to Him. As the *archegos,* He leads us into that eternal salvation. In this way He is the Captain of Salvation, the Prince of Life, and the Pioneer (Author) of our Faith.

MEDIATOR

Jesus is also called the "mediator" by the Apostle Paul (I Timothy 2:5; cf. also Hebrews 8:6; 9:15; 12:24). In the first century this was both a legal and commercial term. It differs from Christ's title as our "Advocate" in that the "Mediator" is impartial; He represents both parties equally. Only Jesus could be the mediator between God and man because only He is both God and man. The Greek word *mesites* literally means "a go-between" and is used in two ways in the New Testament. First,

Jesus is the Mediator in that He mediates between God and man to effect a reconciliation (I Timothy 2:5). Secondly, He is the mediator of a better covenant (Hebrews 8:6), the new testament (Hebrews 9:15), and the new covenant (Hebrews 12:24) in the sense that He acts as a guarantor so as to secure that which would otherwise be unobtainable.

CONCLUSION

No wonder the hymn writer exclaimed, "I will sing of my Redeemer"! The more we understand what the Bible describes as "so great salvation," the more we appreciate the salvational names of Jesus. Some of them speak of His work in saving us. He is "the Redeemer," "Saviour," and "Mediator." Others speak of His Person in saving us. He is "the Lamb of God" and "the Propitiation for Our Sins." Still others mysteriously reveal the One who both produces and is our salvation. He is "the Last Adam," "the Second Man," and "the Author of Eternal Salvation." All of our questions concerning our salvation are answered in His names.

But, the meaning of His salvational names ought to be applied to our lives. He is the propitiation for the sins of the whole world, but we may call Him "my Propitiation" only when we have received by faith that payment for sin. He is our "Mediator" in the deepest sense when we believe on Him as Saviour. Knowing the salvational names of Jesus carries with it a grave responsibility—that of being certain we have obtained so great a salvation. And if we have, knowing the salvational names of Jesus provides for us a tremendous privilege, for we can introduce others to the One who loves us and gave Himself for us.

For Discussion:

1. From what has Christ redeemed us? What was the payment or ransom?

2. Why was the name Saviour neglected by the apostles? How can we avoid taking this title and work of Christ for granted?
3. How should we feel and act in response to Jesus' work as the Lamb of God?
4. When Christ is called Propitiation, what has He accomplished? What influence should this have on our lives?
5. Why is Christ called the last Adam? Are you under the headship of the first or last Adam?
6. Give as many titles of Christ as possible that relate to our salvation. Discuss briefly what each title suggests about salvation.

CHAPTER SIX
THE BIRTH NAMES OF CHRIST

"Therefore the Lord himself shall give you a sign: Behold, a virgin shall conceive, and bear a son, and shall call his name Immanuel" (Isaiah 7:14).

"For unto us a child is born, unto us a son is given: and the government shall be upon his shoulder: and his name shall be called Wonderful, Counselor, The Mighty God, The Everlasting Father, The Prince of Peace" (Isaiah 9:6).

The virgin conception of Christ was prophesied many years before His birth in Bethlehem and, when understood correctly, is one of the foundational doctrines of Scripture. Genesis 3:15 is the first reference to the coming of Christ; embryonically it anticipated the virgin birth by calling Jesus "the seed of the woman." The miracle of the virgin birth was not so much in the birth but, rather, in the supernatural conception of Jesus. There are five persons in Scripture with supernatural origins. Adam was created with neither male nor female parents. Eve's origin involved a man but no female. Isaac was born to parents both of whom were beyond the age in which they could physically produce children. John the Baptist was born to parents who were well into old age. But the greatest of the supernatural origins was that of Jesus, whose birth involved a virgin but no man.

As miraculous as the virgin birth of Jesus Christ was, the real significance of the event is that it marked the incarnation of Christ. In the words of John, "the Word was made flesh" (John 1:14). Even Isaiah, the prophet of the virgin birth, alluded to the incarnation when he differentiated between a human child born and the divine Son given (Isaiah 9:6). The birth of Christ, celebrated each year at Christmas, marks the time when He emptied Himself to become a man. Though He always remained God, while on earth, the glory of Jesus was veiled, and He chose voluntarily to limit Himself in the independent use of His non-moral attributes.

One of the tasks of the parents of a newborn baby is to give that child a name. Usually the parents will spend several months discussing possible names they may or may not choose. Often friends and relatives will suggest names they think are suitable. I have often suggested that expectant parents consider naming a son "Elmer," so far without success! The concern of many parents is to choose a name that expresses their aspirations for their child or suggests by association a positive role model for the child. When that name is chosen, it has a special significance to the proud parents of the newborn baby.

Several of the names and titles of Jesus were given in the context of His birth. It is almost as though the prophets of God sought for the ideal name for the baby Jesus as they anticipated His coming to this world. In this chapter, we propose to look at several of what may be called the "Birth Names of Jesus."

THE DAYSPRING FROM ON HIGH

When Zacharias prophesied at the birth of his son John, he called his son "the prophet of the Highest" (Luke 1:76). But the emphasis of his prophecy focused upon the One whom he called "the dayspring from on high" (Luke 1:78). It was to be characteristic of the life and ministry of John that he, "a bright and shining light," should seem dim in comparison to his cousin, who was the "Light of the World."

The word "Dayspring" is a translation of the Greek word *anatole*, literally meaning "a rising of light" or "sunrise." The place of the dayspring was the point along the eastern horizon at which the sun rose, a place which constantly changed with the passing seasons (cf. Job 38:12). By implication, the term came to mean the east—that is, the direction of the sunrise (cf. Matthew 2:1). Zacharias used it metaphorically of Christ, the One through whom the true Light shone, not only to Israel but to all the world.

But there is something unique about this particular sunrise. This dayspring originated "from on high" *(ex hupsos)*. *Hupsos* refers not only to height but to the idea of being raised to a high or exalted state (cf. James 1:9). It closely relates to the adjective *hupsistos*, the word which describes John as the prophet "of the Highest" (Luke 1:76). The use of this particular term in this context implies that this was uniquely a divinely appointed or exalted sunrise. Perhaps the sun shone just a little brighter on the morning following the birth of the Dayspring from on High.

The appearance of the Dayspring from on High on the horizon of human history produced significant effects. Its shining exposes our sin. Its warmth revitalizes our hope in sorrow. And its light redirects our steps.

The Revelation of Our Sin

In speaking of the visitation of the Dayspring from on High, Zacharias suggested His purpose, "To give light to those who sit in darkness" (Luke 1:79). One of the effects of a natural sunrise is the illumination of an otherwise dark world. Someone has observed that the darkest hour of night comes just before the dawn. There is certainly a spiritual reality in the application of this truth. The Greek word *skotia* is used in the New Testament not only of physical darkness but also of the spiritual darkness of sin. Of the various Greek words that describe darkness, this word indicates the darkest. So, the effect of sin in the life results in not a mere gloominess but a blinding darkness in which any measure of illuminating light is absent. So dark is the darkness of sin that even sin itself is hidden by the darkness.

The cresting of the sun over the mountains along the eastern horizon first makes visible the shadows in the night and then that which the shadows hid in the night; so, the appearance of the Dayspring from on High produces first the light of conviction in a soul darkened by sin and then floods the soul with gospel light, so that we can understand spiritual truth (II Corinthians 4:4-6). When Jesus was challenged to pass sentence upon the woman caught in the act of adultery, He merely spoke the word that brought conviction to the conscience of each accuser (John 8:9). In that place John uses the verb *eleochomenoi,* translated "convicted" but literally meaning "to bring to light and expose." Just as one might hold a letter up to the light to expose its contents, so Jesus exposed the sin of self-righteous people by His penetrating light.

Our Revitalization in Sorrow

There is yet another effect of the natural sunrise which finds a spiritual counterpart in the Dayspring from on High. The light and warmth of the early morning sun is that which revitalizes life on earth. As the light of the sun rises on the eastern horizon, the flowers of the field once again turn and open to absorb the benefits it offers. The animals which hid from the darkness and dangers of the night begin to come out of the caves and hollow logs to enjoy the day. The people of primitive lands begin to remove the coverings which kept them warm in the night as the sunlight of a new day announces yet another opportunity to work while it is still light. It is, therefore, not without significance that Zacharias should note the shining of light to those who walked in "the shadow of death" (Luke 1:79).

Light was one of the great symbols of Messianic prophecy. According to Isaiah, the Messianic light was to shine brightest in Galilee of the Gentiles, upon people who walked in darkness (Isaiah 9:1,2). Often those who find themselves hiding in the shadows are the ones who benefit most from the light. Darkness aids the criminal in the successful accomplishment of his crime. For that reason people all over the world fear the night and eagerly await morning. The pilgrims of Israel understood the significance of the coming morning and the greater significance of their coming Lord. As they sang their hymns of worship, they testified, "My soul waiteth for the Lord more than they that watch for the morning: I say, more than they that watch for the morning" (Psalm 130:6).

In our sorrow, pain, and hurt the Dayspring from on High shines its revitalizing light and warmth. How often has the discouraged Christian, groping in the shadows of even death itself, found in that heavenly sunrise the source of strength he needs to continue? How encouraging the thought that in our constant struggle with the darkness of this world, the Dayspring from on High shines a light which the darkness cannot hide. French theologian Frederic Godet used to think of the Dayspring in the context of an eastern caravan which had lost its way in the night but, while sitting down and expecting death, soon noticed a star begin to rise over the horizon, providing the light which would lead them to the place of safety. Unquestionably, there are and will be many times in life when, like those discouraged traders, the believer would resign to defeat but for the appearance of the morning light from Heaven.

The Redirection of Our Steps

A third benefit of the appearance of the Dayspring from on High is the redirection of our steps, "to guide our feet into the way of peace" (Luke 1:79). The implication is that the light of the sunrise enables us to see how to walk a straight path that leads to "the way of peace." "A man's heart deviseth his way: but the Lord directeth his steps" (Proverbs 16:9). That our steps often need redirection is self-evident to any and all who have attempted to live the Christian life. The Word of God is the instrument God uses to give direction in our lives (Psalm

119:105). As we continue to walk by faith in the Christian life, we come to know experientially not only "the peace of God, which passes all understanding," but also the God of peace Himself (Philippians 4:7,9).

The Redemption of Our Souls

The priority in the life of John the Baptist was "to give knowledge of salvation unto his people by the remission of their sins" (Luke 1:77). But that was possible only because of the visitation of the Dayspring "through the tender mercy of our God" (Luke 1:78). "The tender mercy of God" is literally "the mercy of the bowels or heart of God," meaning that mercy which springs from the innermost seat of His self-existence. In that mercy the benefits of our individual and corporate redemption are found. Zacharias is concerned both with the national deliverance of Israel (Luke 1:68-75) and the personal salvation of those who come to Christ by faith (Luke 1:76-79). Both of these aspects of salvation will materialize by a visitation from the Dayspring.

The Scriptures view a visitation of God either positively or negatively. When God visits a people in His wrath, it is a time of great and severe judgment. When God visits a people in His mercy, it is a time of salvation. Like the psalmist, our prayer must be, "O visit me with thy salvation" (Psalm 106:4).

How penetrating is the light of that brilliant heavenly sunrise! It reaches into the darkest areas of our life, revealing our sin. When convicted of sin by that light, we begin to understand its horror and the inevitable penalty—death itself. But that is also the light which revitalizes us in our sorrow. If we were to respond to that light while we remain in our darkness, we would no doubt stumble and fall or miss the narrow way altogether, and so it is the same sunrise which provides the light to redirect our steps. The ultimate effect of that light is the redemption of our souls. Understanding and experiencing these few benefits of the Dayspring from on High will cause our hearts to praise and worship the God who granted to us this merciful visitation.

IMMANUEL (EMMANUEL)

When God gave the faithless Ahaz an opportunity to ask Him for a sign to encourage his faith, he was so apathetic to the things of God as to refuse to accept the gracious offer. But the purpose of God would not be defeated. Ahaz was given a sign he would not behold because he chose not to ask for a sign which God had offered to him. "Behold, a virgin shall conceive, and bear a son, and shall call his name Immanuel" (Isaiah 7:14). That unusual name for a son captured the highest of ideals in the religious life of the pious Jew. It was an affirmation of the highest of blessings, "God with us."

Whenever God called a person or group to a seemingly impossible challenge, He reminded them of His all-sufficient promise, "Certainly I will be with thee." Moses was to deliver Israel from Egypt, but God was with him (Exodus 3:12). Joshua was to conquer the promised land, but God was with him (Joshua 1:5). Throughout Israel's history, every effective judge and king owed his success to the fact that "the Lord was with him." When Nebuchadnezzar looked into the fire, expecting to see the flames consuming the physical remains of three faithful Hebrews, he saw them surviving the flames, and the Lord was with them. When the remnant returned to rebuild the temple, they were motivated to action by the prophet's reminder, "I am with you, saith the Lord" (Haggai 1:13).

In contrast to the Old Testament promise of the presence of God, the absence or withdrawal of this presence, when noted, is a foreboding warning of disasters to come. Cain went out from the presence of the Lord to found a society so degenerate God had to destroy it with a flood. Samson woke in the lap of Delilah, not knowing that the Spirit of the Lord had departed, and he was captured by the Philistines. Because of his constant disobedience to the revealed will of God, Saul lost his unique relationship with the Holy Spirit, and God replaced His Spirit with an evil spirit.

But in the New Testament, that relationship between God and man changed and intensified. The Christian has an unprecedented relationship with God in Christ. In this regard, the name Immanuel (Emmanuel) signifies something special in the Christian's life.

First, it is an incarnational name. "The Word was made flesh, and dwelt among us" (John 1:14); in a unique way in human history, it was "God with Us." Secondly, it is a dispensational name. The "in Christ" and "Christ in you" relationship is unique to this present dispensation of grace.

The Effect of Immanuel

In every art and industry of mankind, Christians have found a place where their relationship with Christ can be both enjoyed and expressed. The presence of God is effective, first, in producing a deeper communion with Christ. The Christian life may be summarized theologically in two areas of experience—the point of salvation and the process of sanctification. Before salvation, Christ is present knocking at the door (Revelation 3:20) and waiting to be received (John 1:12). In sanctification, Christ is present dwelling within (John 14:23) and continuously completing the work He began at conversion (Philippians 1:6).

The "God with Us" relationship is effective also in securing a definite conquest with Christ. The Christian is engaged in a spiritual warfare which cannot be waged, much less won, without Immanuel, the presence of God with us. As Joshua prepared to conquer the promised land, a type of Christian experience, he was first assured of the presence of God (Joshua 1:5). In describing Joseph being tempted unsuccessfully by Potiphar's wife, the Scripture is both prefaced and concluded with the remark, "The Lord was with Joseph" (Genesis

71

39:2,21). We are victorious in Christ because Christ is in us working (Philippians 2:13), and we are in Christ winning (Romans 8:37).

Thirdly, a deep consolation in Christ flows from the Immanuel promise. Scripture gives the promise of the presence of God as an assurance to the perplexed (Genesis 28:15), an encouragement for the servant (Exodus 3:12), a fortification for the timid (Jeremiah 1:8), a confidence for the teacher (Matthew 28:20), a rest for the pilgrim (Exodus 33:14), and a strength for the fearful (Hebrews 13:5,6).

The Experience of Immanuel

There is an important distinction between the believer's union with Christ (which exists as a result of the baptism of the Holy Spirit and Christ's work on the cross, both applied at salvation) and the believer's communion with Christ, by which he experiences and enjoys the results of that union. We enjoy the benefits of the name Immanuel—God with Us—as we respond in obedience to the multifaceted call of Christ in our lives.

The first aspect of the call is the call to salvation. Throughout the New Testament, this call has a universal appeal; for God "will have all men to be saved, and to come unto the knowledge of the truth" (I Timothy 2:4) and, therefore, "now commandeth all men everywhere to repent" (Acts 17:30, cf. also II Peter 3:9).

Secondly, there is a call to sanctification. By sanctification God sets us apart to holiness. It involves all three aspects of Biblical separation (cf. I Thessalonians 1:9). First, we are separated to God. Further, we are separated from sin. Finally, we are separated to service. Christ is present with us both in our personal sanctification (John 17:16-23) and our corporate sanctification as a body of believers (Matthew 18:20).

We are also workmen together with Christ (I Corinthians 3:9). God has a specific call to service for every believer. Not every believer has the same calling, but each has the same responsibility to serve in the place of his calling. Scripture describes three aspects of the call. Concerning its source, it is a "heavenly calling" (Hebrews 3:1). Concerning its character, it is a "holy calling" (II Timothy 1:9). Concerning its challenge, it is a call to excellence or a "high calling" (Philippians 3:14).

A final aspect of the call of God is one which most believers prefer to minimize—the call to suffering. Suffering is a very real part of the experience of the Christian life (cf. I Peter 2:19-21). There are two extreme positions to be avoided in this area of the Christian life. First, some run from any and all opposition and hardship and, in doing so, often hinder the testimony of Christ and fail to learn what God is trying to teach them in their suffering. A second group seems committed to multiplying their sorrows to the same effect of hindering the testimony of Christ and at times even resisting the will of God when God wants to bless them. Note the five areas of suffering in the Christian life in which Immanuel becomes particularly meaningful—infirmities, reproaches, necessities, persecutions, and distresses (II Corinthians 12:10).

WONDERFUL

Another of the birth names of Christ is "Wonderful." This title was first used in an appearance of the angel of the Lord to the mother of Samson (Judges 13:8-22) and later was one of the five titles Isaiah ascribed to the "son," "given" and the "child" "born" (Isaiah 9:6). Although many contemporary writers tend to view this Isaiah list as four compound names, the first being "Wonderful Counsellor," the Hebrew word used by the prophet is a noun and not an adjective. Also, the names "Wonderful" and "Counsellor" both appear independently elsewhere in Scripture as names of Christ.

A Definition of His Wonder

This word "wonderful" is used in three different senses in the Old Testament. First, a wonder is something marvelous or spectacular. The expression "signs and wonders" is a common Old Testament designation of the miraculous. The New Testament reserves this designation for miracles of the most incredible variety. They were the kinds of miracles that left the witness with a feeling of wonder (cf. Matthew 15:31; Mark 6:51; Luke 4:22).

A second aspect of this word "wonder" is something mysterious or secret. F.C. Jennings has commented on this name of Christ: "It both expresses and hides the incomprehensible." In this way the name is closely related to the "name written, that no man knew, but he himself" (Revelation 19:12). Even when this name has been thoroughly studied, an element of mystery will still remain about all that it represents in Jesus.

Thirdly, that which is wonderful is separated from the common and belongs to the majestic. It falls in a class all by itself far above the common or ordinary. Charles Haddon Spurgeon suggested, "His name shall be called the separated One, the distinguished One, the noble One, set apart from the common race of mankind."

A Recognition of His Wonder

Jesus is called "Wonderful" because He is wonderful. He is wonderful, first, in his identity. Theologians today can analyze the nature of the *kenosis,* the incarnation, and the hypostatic union of two natures, but after all is said and done, a deep mystery about His Person remains. He is wonderful, further, in His industry. Whether in His work of creation or His work of redemption, all that Jesus did to accomplish His work was wonderful in the sense that the observer of the act or finished work feels overwhelmed with a sense of wonder. Christ was wonderful in His ministry to the extent that the multitudes marveled at the content of His message and the authority of His delivery.

Finally, He was wonderful in His destiny. Born in a barn on the backside of Bethlehem, the legal son of a humble carpenter, His closest associates a group of former fishermen, patriots, and traitors to their country's ideals, His humiliating death between two thieves and His hometown reputed to be "the city of garbage," this Jesus of Nazareth is destined some-day to be declared the King of kings and Lord of lords.

A Response to His Wonder

Charles Haddon Spurgeon once announced to the great crowds who came to hear him preach, "Beloved, there are a thousand things in this world that are called by names that do not belong to them; but in entering upon my text, I must announce at the very opening, that Christ is called Wonderful, because He is so." How do we respond to that wonder?

First, we respond to His wonder with adoration. Jesus ought to be the object of our grateful adoration and worship. Leafing through the pages of an average hymnbook will suggest dozens of suitable expressions of our adoration for Christ.

Secondly, Jesus ought to be the object of our wholehearted devotion. He alone ought to be the object of our deepest and warmest affections. The great commandment of the Law was to love the Lord supremely with one's total being. That also is a valid responsibility of the Christian today.

Finally, we should respond to His wonder by entering into a deeper communion with the One who is called "Wonder-ful." The shallow experience of many Christians today is a sad commentary on their interest in the One who loves them and gave Himself for them. If Jesus is Wonderful, and He is, we should long to spend time with Him in Bible study and prayer and to enjoy sweet fellowship with Christ in all that we do.

COUNSELOR

Another of the birth names of Jesus is "Counselor." The world was brought to ruin by the counsel of the serpent in the garden of Eden. That ruined race can be restored only by another Counselor who advises men in the counsel of God. If Satan is the Counselor of ruin, Jesus is the Counselor of restoration.

The significance of this name of Christ is clear in Scripture by the fact that Christ Himself needs no counsel (Romans 11:33,34); He is described as the fount of all wisdom and understanding (Proverbs 8:14), and is presented as imparting counsel to those who seek it (Psalms 16:7; 73:24; Isaiah 25:1; 28:29). As we study the Scriptures, the qualifications of this Counselor and the quality of His counsel become increasingly obvious. But only when we discern and apply His counsel to life does He become our Counselor.

The Qualification of the Counselor

Most contemporary Christian counselors today affirm there are three basic qualifications of a Biblical and effective counselor. Based upon passages such as Romans 15:14 and Colossians 3:16, they argue that the Christian counselor today must be characterized by a knowledge of the meaning of Scripture as it applies to their personal life, a goodness or empathetic concern for others, and enthusiasm for life and wisdom—that is, the skillful use of Scripture in ministry to others for the glory of God.

If this is what Scripture requires of a counselor, obviously, then, Christ excels in each and every prerequisite. One of His relative divine attributes is omniscience, the fullness of all knowledge. As God, He alone is truly good. He is also the personification of the wisdom of God. He is the Counselor *par excellence,* for He is the only One who fully meets the qualifications of a counselor.

The Character of His Counsel

Isaiah described the nature or character of His counsel with the words "wonderful in counsel" (Isaiah 28:29). A survey of the Biblical references to the counsel of the Lord indicates five aspects of its character.

First, the counsel of Christ sets controls. It controls in the

76

sense that it guides the steps of the believer (Psalm 73:24) and establishes him in that which continues (Proverbs 11:14; 15:22; 19:21; 20:18).

Secondly, the counsel of Christ is creative. It is interesting to note how often the concept of creation stands in close proximity to a reference to the Counselor (Isaiah 40:14,26; Romans 11:34,36). This is an important principle for us to remember. Just because the will of God for someone else in similar circumstances requires a certain course of action does not mean that it is God's will for everyone in that same situation. We must learn to let God be God and be creative in His counsel.

Also, the counsel of the Lord comforts: "Ointment and perfume rejoice the heart: so doth the sweetness of a man's friend by hearty counsel" (Proverbs 27:9). Jesus in His role as Counselor is one of the implications of the name *Paraclete,* which the New Testament applies to Him as well as to the Holy Spirit (I John 2:1, translated "advocate"). In both cases, one of the functions of this One called alongside to help is to encourage the discouraged and comfort the sorrowing.

Fourthly, the counsel of Christ is confidential. This is implied by the Greek word *sumboulos,* used by the LXX translators and New Testament writers (Proverbs 24:6; Isaiah 9:6; Romans 11:34). The term literally means "a confidential advisor." When we seek counsel from the Lord concerning an opportunity or problem, the resulting counsel is confidential, and we do not have to worry about later hearing the subject by the grapevine.

Finally, the counsel of the Lord is corporate. In counseling the Laodicean church to anoint their eyes and improve their vision, Jesus used the Greek verb *sumbouleuo,* meaning "to give advice jointly." The Father as the God of all comfort and the Holy Spirit as the Comforter are the other advisors of the believer. David also called the Scriptures his counselors, for they are the instrument this Trinity of counselors uses to communicate the counsel of God.

The Discerning of His Counsel

How can we discern the counsel of Christ in our lives? Among the many principles of Scripture for discerning the will of God, five stand out predominantly. First, the counsel of God is revealed in the Scriptures (II Timothy 3:16,17). Secondly, this counsel often comes through prayer (Judges 20:18,23; I Samuel 14:37). Third, we discern it from the help of wise counselors (Proverbs 11:14; 12:15; 24:6). Fourth, we recognize it through circumstances. Eliezer was aware of the Lord's leading in his life, and circumstances confirmed this to be so (Genesis 15:2; 24:27). Finally, the Holy Spirit reaffirms it. Paul sought to go several places to preach the gospel which were not where God wanted him to go. Because he was sensitive to the leading of the Spirit, he could discern closed doors and had a deep assurance he was doing what God wanted him to do when the doors finally opened (Acts 16:6-10).

THE MIGHTY GOD

Isaiah also called Jesus *El Gibbor,* "the Mighty God" (Isaiah 9:6). Although He "emptied himself" ("made Himself of no reputation"—KJV) to become a man (Philippians 2:7), Jesus never abandoned His divine attributes. Is it not paradoxical that the Mighty God should clothe Himself as a newborn child? If there is any question about Isaiah's view of this coming child, clearly here he indicates He is God incarnate.

Scripture used the Hebrew word *gibbor,* translated "mighty," not only of God but also of the "mighty men" who were soldiers of Israel distinguished in battle. It conveys the idea of exceptional physical strength and prowess. When used of God in the Old Testament, it expressed the assurance that God would defend Israel from her enemies (Psalms 24:8; 45:3). It emphasizes the relative attribute of omnipotence and suggests God will use that power on behalf of His people.

THE EVERLASTING FATHER

Jesus is also called "the Everlasting Father," or more literally, "Father of Eternity." This is the most emphatic assertion of His deity offered by the prophet Isaiah. This title of Christ has caused some confusion among Christians in trying to understand the mystery of the Trinity. Jesus is not here called the Father as God the Father is the Father. He is a distinct Person of the Trinity. The Persons of the Trinity are equal in nature but distinguishable in Person and distinct in duties.

The title "Father" is used here of Christ in the sense of a "founding father." People will talk about the founding fathers of a country or movement, meaning those persons who were the pioneers of an idea and gave birth to the movement or nation. In this sense, Jesus is the founding father of eternity, existing before it began and giving birth to time and history.

THE PRINCE OF PEACE

Isaiah also calls Jesus "the Prince of Peace." He is a Prince now and will ultimately be recognized not only as a king but as the King of kings (Revelation 19:16). As the Prince of Peace, Jesus can meet the deepest need in the human heart—that of peace with God, with himself, and with others round about him. Peace with God is a result of our justification and based on his shed blood at the cross (Romans 5:1; Ephesians 2:13; Colossians 1:20). He is both the God of Peace (Philippians 4:9) and *Jehovah Shalom* (Judges 6:24).

Notice how these five names suggested by Isaiah relate to the ministry of Christ. He was Wonderful in life as He performed various signs and wonders to demonstrate who He was. He was our Counselor by example and teaching. And He perpetuated His counsel by giving us the New Testament. In His resurrection He demonstrated Himself to be the Mighty God. He ascended into glory as our Everlasting Father, and when He returns, He will do so as the Prince of Peace.

CONCLUSION

When parents choose a name for their child, they often strive to select one which expresses their hopes for what the child will be someday. Parents name children after people whom they admire and respect. When God inspired His prophets to select names for the Christ Child, He had the advantage of omniscience. His names not only expressed desire but affirmed the very nature and character of the Child. Jesus is the Dayspring from on High, Immanuel, Wonderful, Counselor, the Mighty God, the Everlasting Father, and the Prince of Peace. Have you acknowledged Him to be each of these in your life?

For Discussion:

1. Of all the individuals in Scripture with supernatural births, why is the birth of Christ the greatest?
2. How is Christ our Dayspring?
3. How should the name and work of Christ as Immanuel affect our daily lives?
4. Name several ways Christians may express their worship of our "Wonderful" Christ.
5. How and when does Christ counsel the believer?
6. Is Jesus the Prince of Peace today, or is this a future event?

CHAPTER SEVEN
THE SERVICE NAMES OF CHRIST

"Even as the Son of man came not to be ministered unto, but to minister, and to give his life a ransom for many" (Matthew 20:28; Mark 10:45).

Jesus described His ministry here on earth in terms of ministry to others. Although there were times when He was entertained by friends and others provided for His physical necessities, His primary concern was what He could do for others. Wherever He was, He found needs and met them. The crowds followed Him not so much for His dynamic charisma as for what He did for them. They came for healing, to have demons cast out, or to be fed with loaves and fish. Their motives were often less than noble. Jesus met needs in lives, and some people chose to follow Him. Jesus was primarily a minister to others.

When He ascended to Heaven, He continued to be a minister to others. Even today He is primarily interested in meeting the needs of others. Every name of Jesus represents His ability to meet a particular need in someone's life. Sometimes I have asked, "What is the greatest name of Jesus in the Scripture?" Actually, there is no standard answer to that question. The greatest name is the name that meets the greatest need you feel. For some, it is "Jesus," the name that relates so closely to salvation. To others, it is "Christ," the name that relates so closely to victorious Christian living. Someone who is often discouraged might think of the name "Comforter" or "Consolation" as the greatest of His names.

Although every name of Jesus ministers to human needs, some names more characteristically describe Jesus in His role as minister. These names I call "the service names of Jesus." There are many such names in Scripture because His range of ministry is so wide. Our objective in this chapter is to examine only a few of the more prominent service names of Jesus.

When we think of the service names of Jesus, the subject of where Jesus is necessarily arises. Obviously Jesus can serve only in the place where He is. There are actually five aspects to the presence of Christ in Scripture. First, He is omnipresent. This means that, as God, He is at all times in every place wholly present. Then there is a localized presence of Jesus, such as when Stephen saw Jesus standing to greet him as he was being condemned and stoned (Acts 7:55). We also speak of the indwelling presence of Jesus; Christ lives within the believer (Colossians 1:27). A fourth presence of Jesus is the institutionalized presence of Christ. There is a sense in which Christ dwells in the midst of the church (Ephesians 1:22,23). Finally, Christ the incarnate Word dwells in the Scriptures, the Inspired Word; and the Scriptures are, therefore, identified as the Word of Christ (Colossians 3:16).

THE CREATIVE NAMES OF JESUS

When we think of the service names of Jesus, we must begin with those titles which relate to His creation and sustenance of this world. In this regard Jesus is both the Creator and Sustainer of the world and all life therein. The prominent references to Christ in two key Christological passages particularly emphasize this fact.

The first of these is John 1, in which Jesus is introduced as the *Logos*. John affirmed, "All things were made by him; and without him was not any thing made that was made" (John 1:3). In discussing the creative work of Jesus, John uses the verb *egento*, meaning "generated or energized." Jesus created by producing life and energy from nothing. The verse following argues, "In him was life; and the life was the light of men" (John 1:4). Jesus is life.

The second key passage is Colossians 1:15-22. Perhaps no

82

other statement concerning Jesus Christ is as magnificent as this one. Although Jesus is never mentioned by name in this passage, no fewer than fifteen pronouns are used with reference to Christ. "For by *him* were all things created, that are in heaven, and that are in earth, visible and invisible, whether they be thrones, or dominions, or principalities, or powers: all things were created by *him,* and for *him:* and *he* is before all things, and by *him* all things consist" (Colossians 1:16,17). These verses identify Christ as both the Creator and Sustainer of life. The terms "thrones, dominions, principalities, and powers" are generally considered to refer to various rankings of angels. Christ created them all and came before them all. Here Paul is portraying Christ as more than a super-angel, probably in an effort to correct a false teaching in the early church.

The word "consist" (Colossians 1:17) literally means "to hold together." This is similar to John's portrayal of Jesus as life. Energy is the glue that holds this universe and all of its component parts together. God is the source of energy because life begets energy. Scientists have discovered an incredible amount of energy in every atom, but God is the source of that energy. When viewing this aspect of the nature of God, we must be careful not to go to the extreme of Spinoza who defined energy as his god. Although God is the source of energy, we must not think of Him as energy itself.

THE INSTRUCTIVE NAMES OF JESUS

Several names of Jesus in the New Testament emphasize His role as a teacher. It is interesting that the Scriptures never call Jesus a preacher (although that may be implied by the title Prophet), but at least four terms are used to distinguish Him as a teacher. Each of these terms differs slightly in meaning, and together they give a more complete picture of both the nature and emphasis of His teaching ministry.

83

THE NAMES OF JESUS

Rabbi

The word *rabbi* is an Aramaic word which the writers of the New Testament transliterated into the Greek. In many cases, translators have done the same, bringing the word over into the English language letter for letter. It was a common way to address a religious teacher in the first century and was first used to address Jesus by two of his first disciples (John 1:38). In that place John explains to his Greek readers that the title was equivalent in meaning to "Master" *(kurios)*, a common Greek reference to a philosopher or teacher.

The Aramaic word literally means "my great one" and represented the great respect the Jews had for their rabbis. The title included not only the idea of teaching but also a certain content in their teaching. It was used much as we today speak of a charismatic teacher, or a deeper-life teacher, etc. When people addressed Jesus as "Rabbi," they were normally discerning the nature or content of His teaching.

Rabboni

The title *Rabboni* is used only on two occasions to refer to Jesus. It was first used by blind Bartimaeus in his request for sight (Mark 10:51). Later, Mary Magdalene used it upon her recognition of the resurrected Christ. On both occasions it was used by people who had a deep sense of loyalty or affection for Christ because of a major miracle He had performed in their behalf. It is an intensified form of the title "Rabbi" and might be translated "My Rabbi." When Mary used it on that resurrection morning, she no doubt spoke it with deepest love for and commitment to the One who was not just another teacher but the One she would claim to be her own (John 20:16).

Didaskalos

A third instructive name for Jesus is the Greek word

didaskalos, usually translated "teacher" or "master." This was the title Nicodemus used when he addressed Jesus as "a teacher come from God" (John 3:2). It was characteristic of His ministry that the crowds who heard Him teach were astonished at His doctrine or teaching (cf. Matthew 7:28,29; Mark 1:22,27). Although it is popular today to speak of the sermons of Jesus, it would probably be more correct to consider them as his Adult Bible Class lessons, because they refer to Jesus' teaching rather than preaching. Six major blocks of Jesus' teaching are recorded in Matthew, including the Sermon on the Mount (Matthew 5—7), His instructions to His apostles before sending them out (Matthew 10), His parables on the kingdom of heaven (Matthew 13), His teaching on greatness in the church (Matthew 18), His sermon in the temple on the day of testing (Matthew 21—23), and the Olivet Discourse concerning things to come (Matthew 24—25). John includes an additional account of a teaching session of Jesus, the Upper Room Discourse (John 13—16), and several detailed accounts of other lessons. Luke also emphasizes the teaching ministry of Jesus, particularly in recording the various parables He taught.

The teaching of Jesus was unique in both content and style. He taught not the tradition of men as was common in His day but the Word of God. Like the prophets of old, He spoke on behalf of God; but unlike those who prefaced their most authoritative appeals with the remark "Thus saith the Lord," Jesus was unique for His comment, "But I say unto you." He differed from the scribes, the usual teachers of the Law, not only in content but in His style of teaching. When a scribe taught the Law, he announced his text and proceeded to recite all the various opinions of other respected teachers of the Law. Only then did he conclude by announcing the consensus of scholarship on the subject. But Jesus spoke authoritatively with little or no appeal to the usual authorities.

85

Kathegetes

A final name of Jesus which alludes to His teaching ministry is the term *kathegetes,* meaning "guide." It is used only on one occasion in the New Testament, where Jesus urged His disciples, "Neither be ye called masters: for one is your Master, even Christ" (Matthew 23:10). Here this term is twice translated "master" in the King James Version, but other translators have used words like "leader," "teacher," and "instructor" to convey the meaning of this word. It differs from the other words for "teacher" in Scripture in that it conveys the image of a teacher who influences or guides a student not only intellectually but morally. Jesus is unique among teachers in that He alone can teach the truth and lead us most fully in the way of truth.

THE SOVEREIGN NAMES OF JESUS

Several different names of Jesus are translated with the English word "master," including most of the instructive names of Jesus cited above. But at least three titles of Christ include in their meaning the idea of mastery over someone or something. These too are service names of Christ, for they demonstrate His power and authority over others and, therefore, evince His ability to serve.

Epistates

Luke alone uses the Greek word *epistates;* he uses it six times of Christ (Luke 5:5; 8:24-45; 9:33,49; 17:13). It is a strong term, meaning "chief, commander, leader, or overseer." It relates closely to the word translated "bishop" in the King James Version, which is a title of the pastor in a church (I Timothy 3:1). It designates the absolute authority of the one so addressed and would ordinarily be considered an honorable title. It was apparently never used except by a disciple and in every case occurs within a context in which the speaker's view of Jesus is somewhat defective. It is always followed by the user being rebuked for his action or conclusion, or the user experiencing something that causes him to grow in his understanding of who Jesus is.

Oikodespotes

Jesus used the term *oikodespotes* to refer to Himself in several of His parables. It is translated "master of the house" (Matthew 10:25; Luke 13:25; 14:21), "goodman of the house" (Matthew 20:11; 24:43; Mark 14:14; Luke 12:39), and "householder" (Matthew 13:27,52; 20:1; 21:33). This was the usual title for the master over the household stewards. It emphasizes the absolute control of that master over those stewards. Jesus used this title in two contexts. First, He is master over His disciples, who are stewards of the mysteries of God. Secondly, in those eschatological parables in which He used this term in the context of His return, He is master over all mankind. By this title, Jesus claimed absolute authority over men both in this life and that to come.

Despotes

Only once is Jesus referred to by the term *despotes* and that by Peter in his second epistle (II Peter 2:1), where the King James Version reads "Lord." Vine suggests this word refers to "one who has absolute ownership and uncontrolled power." It is perhaps the strongest title of Christ that argues for His Lordship. It was commonly used in Greek to refer to a master who exercised a rigid authority over his slaves and is the root of its English derivative, "despot," referring to any ruler having absolute control, particularly a tyrant or oppressive leader. The negative connotation—abuse of power—is not necessarily implied in this term, only the absolute nature of his authority.

THE ASSISTANCE NAMES OF JESUS

Some of the service names of Jesus can best be described as "assistance names," for their primary emphasis points out how Jesus assists the believer in living the Christian life. The Christian life has been explained as Christ living in and through the Christian (cf. Galatians 2:20). Because this is true, every one of the more than 700 names and titles of Jesus, in a sense, is an "assistance name." But the names considered in this section more properly belong here because of the more direct role the Lord plays in our Christian life, as implied in these names.

The Intercessor

Jesus is our Intercessor; one of His primary works on behalf of the Christian today is that of intercession. The writer to the Hebrews noted, "Wherefore he is able also to save them to the uttermost that come unto God by him, seeing he ever liveth to make intercession for them" (Hebrews 7:25). This is one of the two primary functions of Christ as our High Priest.

The need for an intercessor has long been felt by man. In the midst of his despair, Job cried out, "O, that one might plead for a man with God, as a man pleadeth for his neighbour!" (Job 16:21). He realized man's greatest need was someone who could stand before a holy God on behalf of a sinful human race and pray effectively for that race. That is why he earlier lamented, "Neither is there any daysman betwixt us, that might lay his hand upon us both" (Job 9:33). That missing Daysman was the One whom Paul in the New Testament called "the Mediator" (I Timothy 2:5).

The twofold purpose of the Intercessor's prayer on our behalf is to keep us from sinning and, in so doing, save to the uttermost. Of the two primary ministries of Christ as our High Priest, this is concerned most with preventing problems in the Christian life. The Intercessor is known for what He does; He pleads that we might not sin.

The Advocate

The second of Jesus' ministries as a High Priest is advocacy. Jesus is called "an advocate with the Father" (I John 2:1), meaning that He stands before God on our behalf. As Intercessor, Jesus pleads that we might not sin. As Advocate, He stands by us after we have willfully sinned. John uses the Greek word *paraclete,* meaning "one called alongside to help." This is also a name of the Holy Spirit, translated in another place "Comforter" (John 16:7).

The duty of an advocate is to stand by the person and/or principles which he supports. One legal phrase used today to describe an advocate is "a friend of the court." Years ago when I had to go to court over a traffic accident, my insurance company supplied a lawyer who acted on my behalf. Throughout the course of the case, the lawyer spoke on my behalf to insure that the court heard my side of the traffic accident. Although I did not speak in the courtroom myself, my case was heard and won because of the efforts of my advocate, the lawyer.

Similarly, Jesus acts as our advocate before the Father in Heaven when the devil accuses us of sin. Jesus is the Man in the glory, a priest after the order of Melchizedek, who is both qualified and capable to represent our cause in the court of Heaven. He does not actually have to plead our case every time we sin. His constant presence before the Father is the sufficient plea for our failings. His defense rests upon His work— what He accomplished at Calvary on our behalf.

Because both Intercessor and Advocate are aspects of His work as High Priest, the qualifications for both tasks are the qualifications for the priesthood. To be a priest, one needed the right birth, right calling, and right qualifications. Jesus qualifies to be our High Priest and, therefore, both our Intercessor and Advocate because, after the order of Melchizedek, He was called of God to be our High Priest and was anointed of the Holy Spirit just as priests were anointed with oil to begin their priestly ministry. The Man in the glory (Hebrews 6:19-20 with 7:24) is not only our High Priest but also our Intercessor and Advocate.

The Propitiation for Our Sins

A third of the assistance names of Jesus is "the Propitiation for our sins" (I John 2:1). The Greek word *hilaskomai* means "a satisfaction." It was used by pagan Greeks to describe sacrifices to their gods which were offered as an appeasement to their wrath. In the Scriptures, this word is never used in connection with any act of man that might appease the wrath of God; rather, God is propitiated by the vicarious and expiatory sacrifice of Christ. In the sacrifice of Christ on the cross, the holy and righteous character of God was vindicated, making it possible for Him to be a just God and at the same time to forgive sin. Jesus not only accomplished the task of propitiating the Father but was Himself the propitiation or satisfaction by which God was propitiated.

John describes Jesus as the propitiation for our sins (plural). Earlier in this epistle he used the singular form of the noun "sin" (cf. I John 1:7-8). When the word "sin" appears as a singular noun in this epistle, the apostle is speaking of the sinful nature of man. When the noun is plural, John is speaking of the practice of sin. Jesus not only "cleanseth us from all sin" (I John 1:7) but also forgives us our sins (I John 1:9). He is the sufficient payment or propitiation for the sins we commit—past, present, and future—and not only for our sins "but also for the sins of the whole world" (I John 2:2). The death of Christ was sufficient to save anyone regardless of his history of sin.

The Indweller

Although the title "Indweller" is not found in Scripture, this name for Jesus is Biblical in spirit. The names of Jesus reflect the actions of Jesus, and these acts include indwelling the believer. Many Christians realize the Holy Spirit indwells them but do not know that Jesus Himself also lives within. Jesus promised to "manifest" Himself to His disciples and later explained, "If a man love me, he will keep my words: and my Father will love him, and we will come unto him, and make our abode with him" (John 14:20-23).

The conscious recognition of Christ's indwelling the believer is sometimes called communion with Christ or the deeper Christian life. The condition which the believer must keep in order to enjoy this communion is a deep love for Christ which evidences itself in a willing obedience to do the commands of Christ. We cannot claim to have this kind of love for Christ while we rebelliously resist the Lordship of Christ. Our obedience to the Scriptures is born not out of a legalistic spirit or fear of the consequences of not obeying but, rather, out of an inner desire to please the One we love.

John uses an interesting word to describe the Father and Son making Their abode within the believer. The word *monai*, translated "abode" in John 14:23, occurs only one other time in Scripture, and there it is translated "mansions" (John 14:2). Obviously, John's use of the word here is significant. While Jesus is in Heaven preparing our mansion, we here on earth are providing Him a mansion. If the Lord were to prepare us a mansion similar to the mansion we are preparing for Him, what would our mansion in Heaven be like? When we understand that Jesus is not only in Heaven but also living within, that in itself should be an incentive to holy living.

CONCLUSION

Jesus came not to be served but to serve. In many ways He is still serving us today. When we learn the service names of Jesus, our appreciation of and love for Him increase. But an understanding of the service names of Jesus does more for us than merely increase our love for the Lord. Jesus said, "It is enough for the disciple that he be as his master" (Matthew 10:25). Since Jesus is by name and nature a minister to the needs of others, too, we as His disciples, minister to others in His name.

For Discussion:

1. The service names of Christ which relate to His act of creation are Creator and Sustainer. Discuss each of these roles.
2. What are Christ's instructive names? What can we learn about Christ from each?
3. The sovereign names of Christ describe His role in giving direction to the believer. What can we learn about Christ from each of these names?
4. The assistance names of Christ reveal how Christ supports and helps the believer. Discuss the meaning and work involved in these names.
5. Share your reaction to reviewing these service names of Christ. Which is most meaningful to you? Why?

CHAPTER EIGHT
THE SONSHIP NAMES OF JESUS

"I will declare the decree: the LORD hath said unto me, Thou art my Son; this day have I begotten thee" (Psalm 2:7).

The Father's favorite name for Jesus Christ is "Son." It is an Old Testament name (Psalm 2:7), and it has eternal implications. Christians around the world call Christ "the only begotten Son." On all but one occasion Jesus referred to God as "Father." The exception to this rule occurred when on the cross Jesus asked, "My God, my God, why hast thou forsaken me?" (Matthew 27:46).

In John 5:19-27 Jesus referred to Himself as "the Son" ten times in His comments to the Jews. He affirmed that the Son did only what He had seen the Father do (5:19), that the Son was the constant object of the Father's love (5:20), that the Father had and would continue to reveal all things and greater works to the Son (5:20), that the Son had power to give life (5:21), that the Father had delegated His authority to judge to the Son (5:22), that men should honor the Son as they honor the Father (5:23), that those who do not honor the Son offend the Father (5:23), that the Father sent the Son (5:23), that the dead will rise to life when they hear the Son's voice (5:25), that the Son has life in Himself (5:26), and that the Father has given to the Son authority to execute judgment (5:27). Obviously, "Son" is an important title of Jesus.

Of all the many names and titles of Jesus, perhaps more belong to this family or category of names than to all the others. At least nineteen names in Scripture relate to the Son. These include: the Son of the Highest (Luke 1:32), the carpenter's son (Matthew 13:55), the son of Mary (Mark 6:3), the son of David (Mark 10:47), the son of Joseph (John 1:45), Son (Mat-

93

thew 11:27), his Son from Heaven (I Thessalonians 1:10), My beloved Son (Matthew 3:17), the Son of God (John 1:49), the son of Abraham (Matthew 1:1), the Son of man (John 1:51), the Son of the Blessed (Mark 14:61), the Son of the Father (II John 3), the Son of the freewoman (Galatians 4:30), the Son of the living God (Matthew 16:16), the Son of the most high (Mark 5:7), a son over his own house (Hebrews 3:6), the Son who is consecrated for evermore (Hebrews 7:28), and the only begotten Son (John 3:16).

Although each of these nineteen "sonship names" of Jesus possesses a special and important significance, this chapter will examine only three of the more prominent names closely. Each of these three names is used in John 3 in connection with Jesus' meeting with Nicodemus. Note the phrases "Son of man" (John 3:14), referring to His Messianic office and humanity; "only begotten Son" (3:16), referring to His unique relation to God; and "Son of God" (3:18), having special reference to the divine nature and character of Jesus.

SON OF MAN

"Son of man" is particularly noteworthy because in the Gospels it appears to be the favorite title of Christ for Himself. He never identified Himself as "Jesus" until He appeared to Paul on the Damascus Road and then only one other time to the Apostle John fifty years later (Revelation 22:16). Only once did He call Himself Lord, and that was in quoting from the Old Testament (Matthew 22:43). Over eighty times during His three-and-a-half-year ministry, Jesus called Himself "the Son of man." It is also interesting to note that only Jesus used this term and that no one else ever addressed Him as "the Son of man."

Why was this term Jesus' favorite title for Himself? The answer to this question lies in its Biblical background. The only occurrence of the term in the Old Testament with any significance appears in Daniel 7:13. There it is a title of Messianic expectation. Daniel describes the Son of man in the context of His return and kingdom. This is the only use of the expression in the Old Testament in which it refers to Christ. Other occurrences of the term in the Old Testament have a different sense (cf. Ezekiel 2:1,3,8; 3:1; 4:1; etc.).

Daniel's vision contrasts the kingdom of the Son of man with the succession of world empires symbolically represented as the lion (Babylon), the bear (Medo-Persia), the leopard (Greece), and the fourth beast—described only as "dreadful and terrible" (Rome). When these great powers and kingdoms pass, One "like the Son of man" remains (Daniel 7:13-14). Closely associated with this One are a dominion, glory, and a kingdom which are greater than all that had come before. The Jews expected their Messiah to conquer an existing kingdom (that is, Rome). They refused His Messianic claims when He did not fulfill their preconceived notions about what Messiah must be like and must do. But someday Jesus will receive the kingdoms of the world from God. He will claim them as King of kings and Lord of lords. This aspect of the prophecy still awaits fulfillment.

The context of John 3 suggests a second reason why Jesus may have favored this name over others: "And no man hath ascended up to heaven, but he that came down from heaven, even the Son of man which is in heaven" (John 3:13). When Jesus was born in Bethlehem, He acquired something He had never possessed before—a human nature. Although He remained God, He became also a man; He possessed a complete human nature. Because He wanted to identify with those He came to save, He chose to call Himself "the Son of man." The key verse of the Gospel of Luke affirms, "For the Son of man is come to seek and to save that which was lost" (Luke 19:10).

Jesus referred to Himself as Son of man in three contexts. He was, first, the Son of man in the context of His earthly ministry (cf. Matthew 8:20; 9:6; 11:19; 16:13; Luke 19:10; 22:48). Secondly, He used this title also when describing His approaching death on the cross (cf. Matthew 12:40; 17:9,22; 20:18; Mark 10:33; Luke 9:22; John 3:14; 8:28; 12:23; 13:31). Finally, Jesus used this title in an eschatological context with reference to His second coming (Matthew 13:41; 24:27,30; 25:31; Luke 18:8; 21:36).

THE ONLY BEGOTTEN SON

When someone asked a little boy what he learned in Sunday School, he replied that the lesson was on "God's Only Forgotten Son." He went on to explain how people forgot about Him, and He had to be born in a stable, and later His parents forgot about Him and left Him in the temple. Although the little boy had misheard the title "Only Begotten Son," he was also right about "God's Only Forgotten Son." People today still forget Him as was also common during His life (cf. John 1:10-12).

The name "only begotten Son" (John 3:16) did not originate in the Gospels but, rather, in Heaven before time began. In the first of the Messianic Psalms, David noted, "I will declare the decree: the Lord hath said unto me, Thou art my Son; this day have I begotten thee" (Psalm 2:7). Over the years, several suggestions have been offered as to the "day" in which Jesus was begotten. In order to resolve a doctrinal controversy in the early church, the church fathers coined the expression "eternal generation." When we speak of the eternal generation of the Son, we mean that Jesus was eternally the Son and did not become the Son at His birth, baptism, death, resurrection, ascension, or at any other historical point in His incarnate life. If Jesus became the Son at a point in time, He would not be the eternal Son and, therefore, not related to the Father as the Son from eternity.

We should understand the difference between being begotten and being identified or named as a son. Traditionally, Jews name their sons eight days after birth, at the time of their circumcision. It is not, therefore, unusual that a period of time should exist between the eternal generation of the Son and various times when He was named or called the Son. I have only one begotten son. When my son was born May 8, 1956, we named him Stephen Richard Towns. About ten years later, I heard another man calling his son by several terms of endearment that sounded too effeminate to belong to a boy. Turning to Stephen, I said, "If I ever give you a nickname, it is not going to be something effeminate like that. I would call you something strong, like 'Sam,' a real man's name." For some reason, the name stuck, and to this day my son is known as Sam Towns. He was begotten Stephen Richard Towns in 1956 but called "Sam" in 1966. Similarly, Jesus is called the Son at His birth, baptism, death, resurrection, and ascension, but He was begotten as Son in eternity past.

Two different Hebrew words for "Son" are used in Psalm 2: *ben* and *bar*. Each has its own distinctive meaning, although both are used throughout the Scriptures to identify the male descendant of a father. The first word, *ben* (2:7), refers to that which Christ achieves—that is, His Lordship. As the firstborn, He is the builder of God's spiritual house. The second word, *bar* (2:12), refers to that which Christ receives as heir of all things—that is, His legacy. The first refers to His honor; the latter, to His heritage.

The word "begotten" emphasizes His uniqueness. All who receive Christ by faith are "sons of God" but not in the same sense that Jesus is the only begotten Son (cf. John 1:12). God had only one Son, and He sent Him to be a missionary. To that Son He gave the promise, "Ask of me, and I shall give thee the heathen for thine inheritance, and the uttermost parts of the earth for thy possession" (Psalm 2:8).

This phrase "only begotten Son" occurs on three other occasions in the Gospel of John. John beheld "the glory as of

the only begotten of the Father'' (1:14), noted ''the only begotten Son, which is in the bosom of the Father'' (1:18), and later
identified Jesus as ''the only begotten Son of God'' (3:18). This
uniqueness of the Son is alluded to prophetically in a birth name
given to Him by Isaiah when he distinguished between ''a child
is born'' and '' a son is given'' (Isaiah 9:6). Jesus had both
a human nature (a child born) and a divine nature (a son given).
Neither nature in any way hindered or altered the other nature.
He was the God-man—one Person with two natures. ''Generation'' and ''only begotten'' are the terms which best express
the eternal relationship that existed between the divine Person
of Christ and the divine Person of the Father.

THE SON OF GOD

The Gospel of John primarily purposes to produce faith in
the reader, more specifically, ''that ye might believe that Jesus
is the Christ, the Son of God; and that believing ye might have
life through his name'' (John 20:31). When I first began to study
and teach theology, it used to bother me that Jesus did not more
often call Himself the Son of God and emphasize His deity.
This was especially frustrating when I heard or read the
arguments of liberals who noted Jesus' use of the name ''Son
of man'' and insisted that Jesus never claimed to be God, only
man. It was not until much later that I began to understand why
Jesus did what He did. It is only when you fully understand
the humanity of Christ that you see His deity. Likewise, only
when you fully see His deity can you then see His humanity.

Although some people like to distinguish between the expressions ''God the Son'' and ''Son of God,'' the difference is more
imagined than real. The phrase ''son of'' was a common
Hebraism to denote a relationship in which the ''son'' possessed
the very same nature as that of which he was ''son.'' Even
today, the highest honor a Jew can receive is to be recognized
as ''a son of Israel'' by the Israeli government, meaning that

he is by nature the personification of the true spirit of the nation. The expression "Son of God," therefore, means Jesus is by nature the personification of God Himself: He is of the very same essence as the Father.

When we refer to Jesus as "the Son of God," we do not mean that He is in any way inferior to or less than God the Father. In every respect the name "Son of God" implies that the Son is both co-equal and co-eternal with the Father. This is also true of other forms of this name—such as, "Son of the Blessed" (Mark 14:61), "the Son of the Father" (II John 3), "the Son of the Highest" (Luke 1:32), "the Son of the living God" (Matthew 16:16), and "Son of the most high" (Mark 5:7).

This relationship of Jesus to the Father was not something that Jesus discovered only later in life. As a twelve-year-old boy, He understood He was the Son of God and needed to be about His Father's business (Luke 2:49). This was also reaffirmed at His baptism. When He was dipped into the water by John the Baptist, God "thundered" from Heaven, "Thou art my beloved Son, in whom I am well pleased" (Mark 1:11). When Jesus was tempted by Satan, He did not dispute that He was indeed the Son of God (Luke 4:3,9), and Satan knew full well that Jesus was the Son of God.

Jesus later encountered a demon-possessed person who called Him " Son of the most high God" (Mark 5:7). "God Most High" *(El Elyon)* is the name of God which demons most often used. Satan fell from his exalted position when he attempted to be like *El Elyon* (Isaiah 14:14). Melchisedek used this name to identify the Possessor of heaven and earth (Genesis 14:19). The constant attack of Satan against *El Elyon* often takes the form of destroying or taking possession of that which rightfully belongs to God.

At His trial, Jesus was accused and charged with both insurrection (at the Roman trials) and blasphemy (at the Jewish trials).

He was asked by the High Priest, "I adjure thee by the living God, that thou tell us whether thou be the Christ, the Son of God" (Matthew 26:63). While He hung on the cross, enemies of Jesus mocked Him with statements such as, "If thou be the Son of God, come down from the cross" (Matthew 27:40); and, "He trusted in God; let him deliver him now, if he will have him: for he said, I am the Son of God" (Matthew 27:43).

CONCLUSION

Jesus was not only the Son of man but also the only begotten Son of God. That is what He claimed and taught. That being the case, we must respond to Jesus in one of three ways. If He lied about His identity and knew it, then His attempt at deception was such that He got exactly what He deserved. If He believed He was the Son of God and was deceived Himself, then He should be regarded not as a liar but, rather, as a lunatic on the level of a man who thinks He is a poached egg. If, however, He was telling the truth—that is, if He really was the Son of God that He claimed to be—then we must recognize and worship Him as none other than the Lord of life and very God of very God. Jesus' claim to be the Son of God gives us these three alternatives today. We must all answer the haunting question of Pilate, "What shall I do then with Jesus which is called Christ?" (Matthew 27:22).

For Discussion:

1. Giving Jesus the title Son implies that the first Person of the Trinity is the Father. What do the sonship names reveal about the Trinity?
2. There are 19 sonship titles of Christ. Which three are predominant? Why?
3. Of all His names, which one did Christ use most frequently

in reference to Himself? Why do you think He preferred this name?

4. Why was Jesus called the only begotten Son?

5. The title Son of God reminds us of the deity of Christ. Can a person be saved apart from belief in Christ's deity? Why or why not?

CHAPTER NINE
THE GODHEAD NAMES OF CHRIST

"And Simon Peter answered and said, Thou art the Christ, the Son of the living God" (Matthew 16:16).

Several names of Jesus are commentaries on the character of Christ, His nature, and His attributes. For a complete understanding of who Christ is, we should consider all of His names, but certain names are foundational to Christological considerations. Usually these names appear in the context of an important Christological passage of Scripture or stress some unique aspect or attribute of Christ and/or His relationship to the Godhead. These names describe Jesus as God incarnate, "the Christ of God" (Luke 9:20).

THE WORD

The Apostle John was the exclusive user of the title "Word." Using the Greek word *logos,* John wrote, "In the beginning was the Word, and the Word was with God, and the Word was God" (John 1:1). He also began his first epistle with a variation of this title. There he noted, "That which was from the beginning, which we have heard, which we have seen with our eyes, which we have looked upon, and our hands have handled, of the Word of life" (I John 1:1). The apostle also used a form of the title in describing the return of Christ to this earth: "And he was clothed with a vesture dipped in blood; and his name is called The Word of God" (Revelation 19:13).

Words are indispensable to language. We use them to communicate a message. Without them we could not explain precisely what we mean. A word defines or describes the idea we intend to pass on to others. When the Jews used the word *logos,* they thought in terms of the Wisdom literature of the Old Testament.

Scholars debate whether John borrowed the term *logos* from the Greeks or the Jews. If the term is Greek, there may be numerous philosophical implications. If the term is Hebrew, John may be making reference to the wisdom of God personified (Proverbs, especially chapters 5—8). Probably John calls Jesus "the Word of God" because this phrase is used over 1200 times in the Old Testament to refer to the revelation or message of God, as in the phrase, "the Word of God came to . . . " Jesus Christ was the message, meaning, or communication from God to men. Jesus was everything the written and spoken Word of the Lord was in the Old Testament. Jesus is, therefore, the expression, revelation, and communication of the Lord. He is both the incarnate and inspired Word. The following listing summarizes the primary ideas of John's introduction concerning the Word:

TEN CONCLUSIONS ABOUT THE WORD IN JOHN 1:1-18

1. The phrase "In the beginning" is not a reference to a point in time but a reference to eternity past (1:1).
2. The personality of the Word is evident in that it is capable of individualization (1:1).
3. The Word has active and personal communication with God (1:1,2).
4. There are two centers of consciousness, for the Word was God yet also was "face to face" or "with" God (1:1).
5. The Word has the essence of deity (1:1).
6. The Father and the Word are one (1:1).
7. The Word was the Agent by which God expressed or revealed Himself (1:18).
8. The incarnate Word has a definite continuity with the preincarnate Word (1:1,14).

103

9. As God lived in a tent, spoke in a tent, and revealed Himself in the Old Testament tabernacle, so the Word tabernacled among us (1:14).
10. The incarnation of the Word is the unique revelation of God (1:4).

THE BELOVED

The title "Beloved" occurs only once in Scripture (Ephesians 1:6), although many passages affirm the Father's love for the Son. God called Jesus "my beloved Son" at His baptism (Matthew 3:17), and Jesus repeatedly acknowledged that "the Father loveth the Son" (John 3:35; 5:20; 17:23). Paul notes we are "accepted in the beloved" (Ephesians 1:6). The particularly comforting aspect of this title is the context in which it is revealed. Jesus is the object of the Father's love, and because we are in Christ, we too are the objects of the Father's love.

THE IMAGE OF GOD

The Greek word *eikon,* meaning "image," is twice used in titles of Christ to express His unique relation to God. The word itself denotes an image and involves the two ideas of representation and manifestation. When Paul affirmed that Jesus is "the image of God" (II Corinthians 4:4), he meant Jesus was essentially and absolutely the perfect representation and manifestation or expression of the Father. In another place Paul altered the title slightly by calling Christ "the image of the invisible God" (Colossians 1:15). It emphasizes that Christ is the visible representation and manifestation of God to created beings. Both contexts convey the idea of perfection in that image.

A second closely related title is "the express image of his person" (Hebrews 1:3). This is one of seven such statements in the early verses of Hebrews—all designed to demonstrate the superiority of Christ. Various versions translate it in different ways: "the very image of his substance" (ASV), "an exact representation of his very being" (Rhm), "flawless expression of the nature of God" (Phillips), "stamped with God's own character" (Moffat), "the copy of his being" (Beck), "the exact representation of God's nature" (Swindoll), "the exact expression of God's nature" (Stibbs), "the impress of the Divine Nature" (F.B. Meyer), and "the exact expression of God's very essence" (Barclay). This wide assortment of translations derives from two key Greek words in this title.

The first of these is the word *character,* which is closely related to the verb *charasso,* meaning "to cut, to scratch, or to mark." Originally this word referred to a marking agent, such as a die, and then later to the impression made by the marking agent. It is similar to the English word "stamp," which first referred to the instrument which printed the impression and later to the impression itself. It suggests the idea of an exact representation of the person or the person himself—that is, the distinguishing features or traits by which a person or thing is known (cf. the English word "characteristics"). What the writer of the Hebrews seems to argue by using this title is that as the wax bears the impression of the seal pressed upon it, revealing all the dominant character traits of that seal, even so Jesus Christ bears the impression of God's essential being, revealing all the attributes of God.

The second word in this title is *hypostasis,* which is more of a philosophical than a theological term. Etymologically, it refers to the sediment or foundation under a building but came to be used by Greek philosophers to refer to the essence or real being of a person thought to rest under the surface appearance of the person. It refers to the substance of what we are. Used here of Christ in this context, it is an argument for the deity of Christ, for He is substantially God.

105

ATTRIBUTIVE NAMES

Several character names of Jesus may be classed as attributive names, for in their meaning they focus upon the various attributes of God. These names underscore two of the more prominent attributes—holiness and righteousness.

In several passages Jesus is called the Holy One. The child to be born to Mary was "that holy thing" (Luke 1:35); later the apostles called Him "thy holy child Jesus" (Acts 4:30). On several occasions the apostles referred to the Lord as the "Holy One" (Acts 2:27; 13:36; cf. Psalm 89:18). The primary thought in these designations is that of consecration or being set apart uniquely unto God. The holiness of Christ was a fundamental requirement of the worthy sacrifice for sin. Because of His holiness, we become holy. One of the Biblical titles for the Christian is "saint," which is connected in thought to the idea of holiness.

Righteousness also is a feature in several of the names and titles of Jesus. He is called "the righteous" (II John 2:1), "a righteous Branch" (Jeremiah 23:5), "the righteous LORD" (Psalm 11:7), "my righteous servant" (Isaiah 53:11), "the righteous judge" (II Timothy 4:8), "a righteous man" (Luke 23:47), "righteousness" (I Corinthians 1:30), and "the righteousness of God" (Romans 10:3). As holiness refers primarily to the character of Christ, so righteousness refers primarily to the conduct of Christ. These two titles are closely related because it is impossible to be righteous without being holy. The righteousness of Christ is an expression of His holiness just as righteousness is the spontaneous expression of the saint.

The holiness and righteousness of Christ are best expressed in His sinlessness. I refer to Christ's sinlessness as a four-legged chair, because there are four Scriptures that affirm our Lord "knew no sin" (II Corinthians 5:21), "did no sin" (I Peter 2:22), was "without sin" (Hebrews 4:15), and could not be convicted of sin (John 8:46). Just as a four-legged chair is the most secure in which to sit, these four statements serve to affirm the sinless perfection of Christ.

PRIORITY NAMES

Several names and titles of Christ may be called "priority names," for they emphasize the priority of Christ either in His Person or accomplishment. The Apostle Paul emphasized this concept when he noted "that in all things he might have the preeminence" (Colossians 1:18). Each of the following names refers to the Lord in this sense.

Jesus is called "mine elect" (Isaiah 42:1) or "the chosen of God" (Luke 23:35). This title emphasizes the priority of Christ as the uniquely appointed Servant of the Lord. When we have a job that needs to be done, often we will spend time looking for the most qualified one to accomplish the task. The greater the job, the more diligently we seek out the most capable and qualified person available. We want to be sure that the chosen one is the best available. When God sought to redeem a lost world, only One qualified to complete successfully that task, and God chose Him to do it. When the mockers at the foot of the cross called out to Him as "the chosen of God" (Luke 23:35), they no doubt intended insults in order to add to His suffering. Actually, it was a reminder to the One who at any moment could have called on legions of angels to release Him and destroy His enemies that He was God's Elect, chosen to complete the specific task in which He was then engaged.

Several titles of the Lord include the words, "the firstborn" (Hebrews 12:23). He is "the firstborn among many brethren" (Romans 8:29), "the firstborn of the dead" (Revelation 1:5—"first begotten" in KJV), "the firstborn of every creature" (Colossians 1:15), and the "firstborn son" (Luke 2:7). The emphasis of the Greek word *prototokos,* translated "firstborn" or "first-begotten" in Scripture, is that of a priority in relationships. When used of Christ, it affirms His priority with the Father and preeminence over all creation. It does not imply the idea that He first came into existence at some point of time so as not to be eternal in nature; rather, it is used in the sense that He held a certain superiority of position (cf. Exodus 4:22; Deuteronomy 21:16,17).

Another priority name of Jesus relates to the concept of firstfruits (Romans 11:16; I Corinthians 15:20). The Greek word *aparche* closely relates to the verb *aparchomai,* meaning "to make a beginning," and was normally used in Scripture in the context of the offering of the first part of the harvest. As a title of Christ, it is a guarantee of our resurrection after the pattern of His resurrection. Just as the firstfruits of the harvest assure the farmer that more will follow, so the resurrection of Christ assures us of our future resurrection.

CHRIST OUR PASSOVER

The Apostle Paul urged the church at Corinth to deal with sin in their personal and corporate lives, stating, "Purge out therefore the old leaven, that ye may be a new lump, as ye are unleavened. For even Christ our passover is sacrificed for us" (I Corinthians 5:7). Although Jesus is the fulfillment of all of Israel's typical feasts and sacrifices, the need for personal holiness in Corinth caused the apostle to single out the passover and apply this word to Christ.

The passover feast was so named because of the promise of God which accompanied its first observance, "And the blood shall be to you for a token upon the houses where ye are: and when I see the blood, I will pass over you, and the plague shall not be upon you to destroy you, when I smite the land of Egypt" (Exodus 12:13). The final of the ten plagues in the land of Egypt involved the death of the firstborn son in every home. Israel was instructed to kill a lamb as a substitutionary sacrifice and apply that blood to the doorpost of the home. By midnight "there was not a house where there was not one dead'' (Exodus 12:30). In the homes stained with blood, the lamb was dead. In the homes lacking the bloodstain, the firstborn son of the family was dead.

Sin is destructive and deserving of the death sentence, but Christ our Passover has died in our place. Because of this, we are spared the inevitable consequences of sin. But when we understand this title of Christ and the work of Christ it emphasizes, our natural response is to look inward and begin the process of purging ourselves of sinful attitudes and habits that are a part of our being. To effect this response in us, Christ has given us the Holy Spirit. The fact that some things which are wrong in our life still bother us is an evidence of the work of the Holy Spirit in reminding us of the real nature of sin and what it cost our Passover.

THE ALPHA AND OMEGA

It is impossible for finite language to describe exhaustively the meaning of Christ in His Person and work in a single title or name, but if one comes close, it is the title "Alpha and Omega" (Revelation 1:8). Two other related titles are "the first and the last" (Revelation 1:17) and "the beginning and the ending" (Revelation 1:8). These names are significant not so much for what they say as what they imply. Alpha is the first or beginning letter of the Greek alphabet. Omega is the last or ending letter of the same. The expression should not, however, be limited only to the literal first and last letters of the alphabet, for the expressions were used much as today we speak of "everything from A to Z."

Jesus is everything from the first to the last, the beginning to the ending, the alpha to the omega, A to Z. He is, as the apostle put it, "all, and in all" (Colossians 3:11). These related titles of Christ serve to emphasize His inexhaustibility. What does Jesus mean to you? Perhaps you have passed through a particular experience in which He met an unusual need in your life. Even if you cannot find the specific name or title of Jesus in Scripture to express adequately that meaning, it is covered under these expressions. Before going on in this book, pause again and turn to the back of the book and review each of the more than 700 names of Christ in Scripture. Jesus is all of these and more. One name cannot express all that He is, and over 700 names cannot exhaust what He is.

CONCLUSION

On the day Peter affirmed that Jesus was the Christ of God, he probably did not comprehend all that was involved in the character of Christ. Jesus was uniquely related to His Father as the Beloved and the eternal Word, who was face-to-face with God in eternity past. He was the One whose names suggest the very attributes of God. He was the One who holds preeminence in all things and priority before all. He was God himself, the express image of His Person, and the visible image of the invisible God.

But in the experience of the believer Jesus is even more than that. He is Christ our Passover, the One who died in our place in order to redeem us from the infection of sin. In fact, Jesus is everything to the child of God. He is the Alpha and Omega, the First and the Last, the Beginning and the Ending, and everything in between.

For Discussion:

1. Why is Jesus called the Word? What does this indicate about His character and work?
2. What does "accepted in the beloved" (Ephesians 1:6) mean?
3. As the Image of God, what does Christ reflect? How does this name relate to believers?
4. There are several names of Christ that come from the at-

tributes of God. Discuss how each of these names reflects a different aspect of God's nature.

5. Does the title Firstborn imply that Christ came into existence at some point in time? Why or why not?

6. As the Passover, what does Christ do for the believer?

7. Christ is the Alpha and Omega. He is the beginning and ending of what? In light of this truth, how should we view our trials and struggles?

CHAPTER TEN
THE JEHOVISTIC TITLES OF CHRIST

"Jesus said unto them, Verily, verily, I say unto you, Before Abraham was, I am" (John 8:58).

The Bible records many statements concerning the deity of Christ, but perhaps none were so impressive to the early church as those which identified Him with Jehovah in the Old Testament. Although the name "Jehovah" was used before the time of Moses, it was not until then that God revealed the uniqueness of its meaning (Exodus 6:3). It was the covenant name of God in the Old Testament and a form of the verb "to be" repeated twice. When Moses maintained he did not know the name of God, God revealed His name as "I AM THAT I AM" (Exodus 3:14). Jehovah is the I am. This name is printed in the English Bible by the title "LORD," in which all four letters are capitalized.

"Jehovah" was the most respected name of God in the Old Testament. When scribes were copying the Scriptures and came to this name, they would change their clothes and find a new pen and fresh ink to write the name. They refused even to pronounce the name as they read the Scriptures; they substituted for it the name *Adonai*. As a result of this misguided expression of reverence, considerable debate has arisen over the actual pronunciation of the name. Although most conservative theologians argue it should be pronounced Je-hov-ah, many liberal teachers argue it should be pronounced Yah-weh. It is impossible to resolve this debate now at a time when the name has remained unpronounced for generations. Even if the Hebrew language included vowels, our task of deciding about how to pronounce this name would be difficult. Dialects change within languages over years of use, so that the same word pronounced one way today may sound totally different two hundred years from today. If we did not know the history of the region, it would be hard for us to believe that the original settlers of the Southeastern United States spoke English with a thick British accent. Over the years and generations since they first settled, they have developed their own unique dialect of English. The same thing no doubt happened to the Hebrew language over a long period.

Jesus used the expression "I am" in eight contexts within the Gospel of John in which He revealed something about His character as Jehovah. The Greek words which John used on those occasions, *ego eimi,* emphatically draw attention to their significance. The following listing identifies the eight contexts in which Jesus called Himself "I am" and is the group of names which this chapter discusses:

THE JEHOVISTIC NAMES OF JESUS IN THE GOSPEL OF JOHN

1. I AM the Bread of Life   John 6:35
2. I AM the Light of the World   John 8:12
3. I AM the Door   John 10:9
4. I AM the Good Shepherd   John 10:11
5. I AM the Resurrection and the Life   John 11:25
6. I AM the Way, the Truth, and the Life   John 14:6
7. I AM the True Vine   John 15:1,5
8. I AM . . . I AM   John 4:26; 8:58; 18:5,6,8

THE BREAD OF LIFE

The Jews widely believed they would recognize the Messiah because He would find the lost ark of the covenant hidden by Jeremiah and produce the jar of manna hidden therein. Hence,

Messiah would be identified with manna or bread. Also, the Jews thought that being a Prophet like unto Moses (Deuteronomy 18:15) meant He would produce the bread from heaven. One rabbinical saying declared, "As was the first redeemer, so was the final redeemer; as the first redeemer caused the manna to fall from heaven, even so shall the second redeemer cause the manna to fall." Further the Jews thought that manna would be the food in the kingdom of God. In the Jewish mind, manna excited Messianic expectations.

In light of this cultural context, it is not surprising that those who were one day ready to declare Jesus to be the Messiah should the next day raise the subject of manna. Twice in a meeting with Jesus, they requested that Jesus produce this manna (John 6:30-31,34). In response, Jesus identified Himself as the manna when he declared, "I am the bread of life" (John 6:35). In the discourse in which He revealed this Jehovistic title, Jesus explained He was the bread of everlasting life (John 6:32-34), the bread of satisfying life (John 6:35-36), the bread of resurrection life (John 6:37-47), and the bread of indwelling life (John 6:48-59).

Just as a person eats bread to sustain his physical life, so the Christian must "eat" the Bread of Life to sustain his spiritual life. In His address on the Bread of Life, Jesus used two different verbs for eating, showing two responses to the Bread. First, He used the verb *phagein,* always in an aorist tense and with reference to eternal life (John 6:50,51,52,53). When a person receives Christ as Saviour, he is, in this context, "eating his flesh." This is a reference to "once-and-for-all" salvation. The second verb, *trogon,* is a present active participle, which emphasizes a continual or habitual eating. It was used of munching on fruit, vegetables, or cereals. The change in tense which accompanies the change in verb emphasizes the continual satisfying of a spiritual appetite through constantly or habitually munching on the Bread of Life (John 6:54,56,57,58). If the first act of once-and-for-all eating speaks of our salvation, this constant munching speaks of our uninterrupted communion with Christ.

THE LIGHT OF THE WORLD

On several occasions the religious leaders in Jerusalem tried to destroy Jesus. One attempt involved bringing to Him a woman caught in the act of adultery and calling on Him to pass judgment. It created for the Lord what they thought was an impossible situation. If He condemned her as required by the Law, the people would be disappointed and stop following Him. If He failed to uphold the Law, He was guilty of teaching contrary to Moses and could be thrown out of the Synagogue and stoned for blasphemy. Jesus upheld the Law in its true spirit by bringing conviction to the woman's accusers and salvation to the guilty woman. At the same time He increased His already growing popularity with the common people.

Immediately following that incident, Jesus announced, "I am the light of the world" (John 8:12). That simple statement was rich in meaning in the context in which it occurs in this Gospel. Jesus uttered it in the court of the women, where He had been teaching. At that place were located the four golden candelabra, each with four golden bowls. As part of the previous week's celebration of the Feast of Tabernacles, these bowls had been filled with oil and lighted. Contemporary observers affirmed that the light was so brilliant as to illuminate the entire city of Jerusalem. Those who gathered around Jesus that morning would no doubt still remember the spectacle of the night before.

By calling Himself "the light of the world," Jesus may have been alluding to the cloud/pillar of fire that led Israel through the wilderness. The ceremonial illumination of a temple was a reminder to the people of that cloud/pillar. Most Jews would have considered that phenomenon a theophany, a manifestation of God Himself. If Jesus was thinking of this background, then His claim to be the Light of the World is a clear title to deity.

Jesus may also have been referring to the rising of the sun. He had begun teaching very early in the morning—that is, just before sunrise (John 8:2). By the time Jesus made this claim, the sun would be bursting over the horizon. Because of the mountainous terrain, the sunrise in Palestine is sudden and spectacular. Within an hour, the degree of light changes from the darkest hour of the night to the brilliance of the day. It was this unique sunrise which caused David to compare the sun to "a bridegroom coming out of his chamber" (Psalm 19:5).

Another possible context for better understanding Jesus' statement about the light of the world is that of the Old Testament prophecies which associate the coming of the Messiah with light. On the preceding day, Nicodemus' colleagues in the Sanhedrin had mildly rebuked him with the statement, "Search, and look: for out of Galilee ariseth no prophet" (John 7:52). It may be that Jesus called Himself "the light of the world" in order to remind these Jewish leaders of very important prophecies they seemed to have forgotten (Isaiah 9:1; 42:6; 49:6; 60:1-3; Malachi 4:2). These prophecies concerning the light specifically named Galilee as the place in which the light would particularly shine.

One other context clarifies the sense in which Jesus is uniquely the Light of the World. Jesus is the light that repels the sinner who will not repent of his sin but that attracts those sinners who will. In the confrontation prior to this statement, Jesus spoke so as to bring conviction to the self-righteous Jewish leaders who had sought to exploit the woman caught in the act of adultery. The word John uses in this context for "convicted" is *elegchomenoi,* literally meaning "to bring to the light and expose" (John 8:9). It describes the act of holding a letter to a lamp so as to see what was inside. Jesus was the Light of the World in the sense that He could hold up men's lives to

116

the light to expose the sin hidden deep within. When He convicts of sin and men are not willing to repent, they cannot remain in His presence. Many people today are trying to run from God because they are convicted of some sin for which they will not repent.

Jesus is the Light of the World, and one of the primary functions of light is to shine so as to reveal what was otherwise hidden. Christ shines to reveal Himself (John 8:12-20), the Father (John 8:21-27), and the cross (John 8:28-30). He not only exposes the hidden sin in man but shows him how the sin problem can be ultimately resolved. He is the light in a world of moral darkness.

THE DOOR

When Jesus identified Himself as the door, He was comparing Himself to the purpose or function of a door (John 10:9). A door was the means by which the sheep entered into the fold. By way of application, Jesus is the door to the fold of salvation. In this context, He emphasizes the exclusiveness of Himself as Saviour by using the definite article *he* ("the") and by identifying salvation exclusively with entering into the fold through that door. The Greek expression *di'emou* ("by me") stands in an emphatic position so as to identify clearly the door by which men may find salvation.

There are at least three specific applications of this particular title of the Lord in the Christian life. "I am the door: by me if any man enter in, he shall be saved, and shall go in and out, and find pasture" (John 10:9). First, Jesus the Door provides salvation when we enter. Secondly, we have liberty to go in and out—in for salvation and out for service. Thirdly, we shall find spiritual food in Him.

THE GOOD SHEPHERD

Jesus twice identified Himself as "the good shepherd" (John

117

10:11,14). In doing so, He used the Greek word *kalos,* which carried with it certain moral overtones. In classical Greek, this word was used to describe that which was beautiful, useful, auspicious, noble, wholesome, competent, and morally good. It would be correct to use any or all of these adjectives to describe the Good Shepherd. This word emphasizes the essential goodness of the Shepherd which, because it is evident to the observer, results in the Shepherd's being admired, respected, and loved by others.

Many commentators believe this title is a reference to *Jehovah Rohi* of the Twenty-Third Psalm. The primary emphasis of the title, however, is the Shepherd's giving His life for His sheep and, therefore, is probably better understood within the context of Psalm 22, the first of the trilogy of Shepherd Psalms (Psalms 22—24). The title "Shepherd" was a church name of Jesus, for Scripture occasionally identifies the church as the flock of God (I Peter 5:2).

THE RESURRECTION AND THE LIFE

When Jesus met with Martha just prior to the raising of her brother Lazarus from the dead, He introduced another of His Jehovistic names. "Jesus said unto her, I am the resurrection, and the life: he that believeth in me, though he were dead, yet shall he live: And whosoever liveth and believeth in me shall never die" (John 11:25,26). Martha had expressed her faith in the resurrection as a principle, but Jesus revealed to her the resurrection as a Person, that Person being Himself. One of the titles of Christ is "Life," and Jesus is the resurrection because He is life in its fullest sense.

This title carries with it a twofold promise for the believer. First, those who have experienced physical death shall rise to immortality. Second, none who believe shall be hurt in the second death. Although we commonly hear this title of Christ at funerals where these promises are repeated, they are condi-

118

tional promises, and this name for Christ has meaning and benefit only to those who believe.

THE WAY, THE TRUTH, AND THE LIFE

Alone with His disciples on the last night of His life here on earth, Jesus revealed two additional Jehovistic titles. The first of these is "the way, the truth, and the life" (John 14:6). The Greek word *hados* literally means "road" or "highway." In the context of the language of a journey, Jesus is the highway to Heaven. Further, He is the only highway to Heaven. The New Testament consistently teaches an exclusiveness with respect to Christ as the only Saviour. Christ claimed to be the only Saviour (John 14:6), and the disciples acknowledged it also (Acts 4:12). This description of Christ was so characteristic of the nature of New Testament Christianity that followers of Jesus were described as being "of the way" or "this way" (Acts 9:2; 19:23; 22:4; 24:14,22).

Christ was not only the way but also the truth in its most absolute nature. He is the fountain and standard of truth. This was important to the Jews. One Jewish legend reports a group of rabbis were praying in order to determine the essential nature of God when God sent a scroll down from Heaven with the first, middle, and last letters of the Hebrew alphabet on it. These three letters spell the Hebrew word for "truth." Although the story is no doubt apocryphal, it does serve to illustrate the importance of truth to the Jews, especially as an attribute of God.

And Jesus is the life. He is unique among men in that He has life in Himself. He is described in the context of His resurrection as a "quickening" or life-giving spirit (I Corinthians 15:45). Life is fundamental to His being and is described early in the fourth Gospel as the life which was the light of all men (John 1:4).

THE TRUE VINE

The second Jehovistic title Jesus revealed that night in the

Upper Room was "I am the Vine" (John 15:1,5). Vineyards were so plenteous in Israel that the vine became a national symbol. A golden vine had been engraved over the temple-gate area, and it had been used on coins minted during the Maccabean revolt. Throughout the Old Testament, God had used the image of a vine or vineyard to describe the nation (Psalm 80:8; Isaiah 5:1-7; Jeremiah 2:21; Ezekiel 15; 19:10; Hosea 10:1). When Jesus called Himself the true vine, He was obviously drawing a parallel between Israel and Himself.

The Greek word *alethine,* meaning "true," is repeatedly used in the Gospel of John to distinguish the reality and genuineness of Jesus in contrast to that which is false and unreal. Although in the Old Testament God often talked of Israel as a vine, the image always appears in a negative sense. In contrast, Jesus is the real or genuine vine, a vine that is cared for and carefully pruned by the husbandman and a vine characterized by consistent fruit-bearing. Israel was never a vine like this; the nation was a spurious vine that produced sour grapes.

I AM . . . I AM

The Greek expression *ego eimi* is used in the context of each of the above Jehovistic claims of Jesus. Simply using the verb *eimi* would have been enough if Jesus had wanted only to draw a parallel between Himself and something else, but the addition of *ego* to this expression draws attention to emphasis. On several occasions Jesus used the expression which includes an emphatic subject and verb but failed to supply the predicate (cf. John 4:26; 8:58; 18:5,6,8). This was not a failure on the part of Christ to complete a sentence but, rather, an affirmation of His being Jehovah (cf. Exodus 3:14). On at least one occasion His statement was understood by those who heard it in this light, for they responded by picking up stones to kill Jesus for blasphemy (John 8:58-59). On another occasion, the uttering of this name was apparently accompanied by a revelation of His glory, which caused the soldiers who had come to arrest Him to fall back under His power (John 18:5-8). Jesus used this expression not just to assert His claims to be *like* Jehovah but to demonstrate that He *was* Jehovah.

CONCLUSION

Jesus is the Jehovah of the Old Testament. All of the names of Jehovah in the Old Testament, therefore, may be applied legitimately to Him (see appendix). He is the eternal contemporary who meets our every need. G. Campbell Morgan once suggested that we could better understand experientially the name Jehovah, I Am, if the verb "to be" were translated "to become." The significance of this name is that Jehovah (Jesus) is and will become to us exactly what we need when we feel that need. In this sense, it is an intensely personal and subjective name of Jesus. What has Jesus become to you recently?

For Discussion:

1. What is important about the I AM's of the eight Jehovistic titles of Christ? How do they reflect His deity?
2. What is the purpose of bread? How does Christ fulfill this purpose for believers?
3. What did Christ mean when He described Himself as light?
4. Relate the function of a door to Christ's ministry. What does it mean to go in and out?
5. How is Christ a good shepherd?
6. What twofold promise is extended because of Christ's title of Resurrection and Life?
7. When Christ said "I am . . . I am," what did He imply? What do we know about Christ because of these Jehovistic titles?

CHAPTER ELEVEN
THE CHURCH NAMES OF CHRIST

"And I say also unto thee, That thou art Peter, and upon this rock I will build my church; and the gates of hell shall not prevail against it" (Matthew 16:18).

Several names of Christ focus upon His unique relationship to the church. The church is described with many metaphors—such as, the body, a flock of sheep, a bride, a temple or building, and a garden or vineyard. In this connection, Jesus is the Head of the Body, the Shepherd of the Sheep, the Bridegroom of the Bride, the Cornerstone and Master Builder of the Building, and the Vine which gives life to the branches.

THE HEAD OF THE BODY

One of the common images of the church, particularly in the epistles of Paul, is the body of Christ. The word "body" is the key word in I Corinthians 12, where the apostle sought to resolve problems at Corinth concerning spiritual gifts. The theme of the Epistle to the Ephesians is the church as the body of Christ (Ephesians 5:23). In the Epistle to the Colossians, probably written at the same time as the Ephesian epistle, Paul's theme is Christ as the Head of the Body (Colossians 1:18).

The "body" is the best known and most used symbol of the church in Scripture. When Paul called Christ "the head of the body," he emphasized the authority of Christ in and over His church. It was a reminder of the distinctiveness and supremacy of Jesus. To comprehend this name more fully, we must understand how the apostle used the word "body" to describe the church.

The Greek word *soma* is used in several ways in the New Testament. On many occasions it refers to the physical body (cf. Romans 1:24; I Corinthians 5:3; Galatians 6:17; I Thessalonians 5:23), but Paul also uses this word to identify the total personality of a man, not just his physical being (cf. Romans 12:1; I Corinthians 13:3, 9:27; Philippians 1:20). It is interesting to note that Paul never uses this word to describe a dead body as is common in Classical Greek and the Septuagint.

Within this context, the church is a living organism, the body of Christ. She has a personality and identity which is intimately related to Christ her head. She is a living entity indwelt by Christ Himself. Although we must be careful not to make the church more authoritative than the Scriptures (as is common in Catholic traditions), it is important that we recognize the living reality of the church as the body of Christ.

If the church is the body, Christ Himself is the head (Colossians 1:18; 2:19; Ephesians 1:22-23; 4:15; 5:23). As the head is the determinative center of one's physical being, so Christ is authoritative in the church. He does not build His church independent of His body but directs and controls the actions of every muscle, organ, and nerve so as to accomplish His will. Part of the mystery of this name is that Christ, who is in His nature and attributes omnipotent, should voluntarily choose to limit Himself to working through human beings who, although they are members of His body, retain an independent will by which they can and too often do refuse the directives of the head.

That Christ is called "the head of the body" implies several truths concerning His relationship to the church. First, it means His purposes cannot be frustrated; He holds ultimate control. Even if one part of the body is rebellious and does not respond to His directives, another will respond. Secondly, it suggests that no individual member within that body can be the organic head of it. Attempts to do so will be frustrated, as in the case of Diotrephes, "who loveth to have the preeminence among them" (III John 9). The place of preeminence in the church belongs to Jesus alone. "And he is the head of the body, the

123

church: who is the beginning, the firstborn from the dead; that in all things he might have the preeminence'' (Colossians 1:18).

The practical implication of this title of Christ relates to our submission to Jesus as the head of the body. He demands our obedience to His will and reverential worship of His Person. Anything less falls short of a personal acknowledgment of Jesus as the Head of the Body.

THE SHEPHERD OF THE SHEEP

Scripture often refers to the church as the flock of God, and so it is not surprising that the Lord should bear the title ''Shepherd.'' When He sees the multitudes of people, He sees them ''scattered abroad, as sheep having no shepherd'' (Matthew 9:36). He was the Good Shepherd in His death (John 10:11; Psalm 22), the Great Shepherd in His resurrection (Hebrews 13:20; Psalm 23) and will be the Chief Shepherd in His return to this earth (I Peter 5:4; Psalm 24). Unlike the hireling whose primary concern is himself, Jesus cares for His sheep. He has entrusted the care of parts of His flock to others called ''pastors,'' or more literally, ''shepherds.'' Jesus the shepherd is the model for pastors in caring for the flock. The title ''shepherd'' was also one of the Jehovistic names of Jesus in the Gospel of John.

THE BRIDEGROOM OF THE BRIDE

When John the Baptist became the first to call Jesus ''the bridegroom'' (John 3:29), the term was already rich in meaning. The Old Testament frequently portrayed Israel as the wife of the Lord (Isaiah 54:6; Jeremiah 31:32; Hosea 2:1-23). As John on that occasion noted, ''He that hath the bride is the bridegroom'' (John 3:29). This title was to have special significance in the New Testament, not for Israel as the wife of God but, rather, for the church, which is the bride of Christ.

The relation between the bride and Bridegroom is most fully taught in a passage in which the Apostle Paul addresses several principles of family living (Ephesians 5:25-27). These verses emphasize that Christ loved the church, gave Himself for it, purposes to sanctify and cleanse it by the Word of God, and promises to take it to Himself as a perfected bride. This work of Christ began in eternity past when He determined to die for her because of his love for her and will be consummated in the new Jerusalem when we shall with John see "the holy city, new Jerusalem, coming down from God out of heaven, prepared as a bride adorned for her husband" (Revelation 21:2).

The image of the bride and Bridegroom serves to emphasize the need for qualitative or spiritual church growth—that is, growth in our love for Christ. The church was "espoused" to Christ by the apostles (II Corinthians 11:2) and should grow closer to Christ during the "engagement period" of this present age. Unfortunately, the history of the professing church suggests she has been as unfaithful to her Groom as Israel was to her Husband.

THE CORNERSTONE AND FOUNDATION OF THE BUILDING

Jesus is called "a stone" or "rock" in three different senses in the Scripture. To Israel He is a "stumbling" stone or "a rock of offence" (Isaiah 8:14,15; Romans 9:32,33; I Corinthians 1:23; I Peter 2:8). To the world He is the smiting stone, which will destroy the antichrist kingdoms of the world (Daniel 2:34). But to the church, "the stone which the builders disallowed, the same is made the head of the corner" (I Peter 2:7). Jesus is the cornerstone of the church, which He is presently building.

Some of the significance of this title has been lost to the average Christian today because of changes in architectural design in the centuries since this title was first applied to Christ.

125

The Greek word *lithos* was used of ordinary field stones that were found on the ground. It was common in the construction of first-century buildings to lean the building into itself. This meant that one part of the structure would have a greater amount of pressure on it than the rest of the structure. Over the years, the materials used in this area would wear faster. To compensate for this, builders sought for a hard field stone upon which the structure would rest. It became known as the cornerstone and was the one part of the building on which the rest of the structure depended absolutely.

When the apostles called Jesus "the cornerstone," they were not thinking of the decorative marble slab affixed to a completed building but, rather, to the foundational rock upon which the building would depend for its stability and strength. In the "temple of God," the church, Jesus is the "head of the corner," which gives both strength and stability to the spiritual temple of believers who are also likened to the stones with which the rest of building is constructed (I Peter 2:5).

THE TRUE VINE AND THE BRANCHES

In the Old Testament, God often used the image of a vine or vineyard to describe the nation Israel (Psalm 80:8; Isaiah 5:1-7; Jeremiah 2:21; Ezekiel 15; 19:10; Hosea 10:1), but always the image was that of an unkempt vineyard which had gone wild. Jesus called Himself, in contrast, the true vine and identified His disciples as the branches of that vine (John 15:1-8). This is perhaps the most intimate of images used in Scripture to describe the oneness of Christ and believers. Jesus is not the stem from which the branches grow but the vine, which is the total life of the branches. The image of a vine is better suited than that of a tree, for the vine and branches grow into one another so that it is difficult to distinguish the vine from the branches. That ought also to be true of the relationship of the believer to His Lord.

This title, "the Vine," is the seventh of the Jehovistic titles of Jesus in the Gospel of John, and further aspects of this title are discussed elsewhere in this book. The practical application of this title to the church relates to our oneness with Christ, the nature of spiritual growth, our responsibility to bear fruit consistently, and the need for occasional pruning.

Because Jesus is the vine and we are the branches, we can accomplish nothing apart from Him. He is the supplier and sustainer of the very life of the believer, and the Christian life is lived by faith in Christ (cf. Galatians 2:20). As He lives His life through us, we will bear fruit. This fruit will consist of both converts to Christ, whom we will be instrumental in reaching; and the character of Christ, which the Apostle Paul describes as the fruit of the Holy Spirit (Galatians 5:22-23). Our primary responsibility relevant to this name of Christ is that of abiding in Him.

From time to time in our Christian lives, we encounter difficult and trying circumstances. Many times they are of the sort which cause us to seek spiritual reasons as to the cause. Many Christians mistakenly conclude at such times that problems in the Christian life are always caused by sin, and even though they may be right with God, they are convinced they have committed some sin which they must have forgotten about. What they fail to realize, however, is that some troubles in the Christian life are the result of our faithfulness. One of the forgotten promises of Christ is that He will reward fruitfulness with pruning that we "may bring forth more fruit" (John 15:2). By using a different metaphor, Job expressed this same hope in the midst of his trial: "But he knoweth the way that I take: when he hath tried me, I shall come forth as gold" (Job 23:10).

CONCLUSION

The above titles of the Lord are significant, for they reveal who He is in relation to His people. This emphasis is so common in Scripture as to be taken for granted too often by Christians. In most religious systems, the deity of that religion is to be feared, served, and sacrificed to. But the Lord delights not in keeping His distance from but in developing a greater intimacy with His people.

Although Jesus does relate individually to His disciples, it is interesting that many of His names should relate to the church. During the sixties, the mood of America was largely anti-institutional, and many Christians were infected with this spirit and rejected the church. Things have changed to some degree since then, but many Christians are still somewhat anti-church. Remember that Jesus loves the church and gave Himself for her and has great plans for her in the days to come. Christians who voluntarily divorce themselves from the church and fail to belong to, support, and pray for their local, Bible-believing church are placing themselves in a position in which they can hardly experience the rich reality of the church names of Jesus.

For Discussion:

1. Discuss the five titles for Christ mentioned in this chapter. What unique ministry is highlighted in each title?
2. How may we express our submission to Christ as the Head of the Body?
3. Discuss how Jesus the Shepherd is the model for pastors in caring for the flock.
4. As a Bridegroom, what does Christ do for those who are His bride?
5. List several contributions that a foundation makes to a building. How do these relate to the believer's life and his cornerstone, Christ?
6. Why does Jesus add the qualifying term "true" when He calls Himself a vine? How does Christ the vine relate to believers as branches?

CHAPTER TWELVE
THE APOCALYPTIC NAMES
OF CHRIST

"The Revelation of Jesus Christ, which God gave unto him, to shew unto his servants things which must shortly come to pass; and he sent and signified it by his angel unto his servant John" (Revelation 1:1).

The final book of the New Testament offers the fullest revelation of Christ in Scripture. Even its divinely inspired title states its purpose as "The Revelation of Jesus Christ" (Revelation 1:1). It is not, therefore, surprising that this book contains over seventy names and titles of Jesus. In reading the Revelation, many people get sidetracked by focusing on obscure symbols or strained interpretations of things to come. But ultimately, when you look at this book, you ought to see Jesus. Note carefully the seventy-two names and titles of Christ in this book. He is called . . .

Jesus Christ (1:1), word of God (1:2), the Faithful Witness, the first begotten of the dead, and the prince of the kings of the earth (1:5), the Alpha and Omega, the beginning and the ending, the Lord, and the Almighty (1:8), the first and the last (1:11), the voice (1:12), the Son of man (1:13), he that liveth (1:18), he that holdeth the seven stars and he who walketh in the midst of the seven golden candlesticks (2:1), he who was dead and is alive (2:8), he who hath the sharp sword with two edges (2:12), the hidden manna (2:17), the Son of God (2:18), the morning star (2:28), he that hath the seven Spirits of God and he that hath the seven stars (3:1), he that is holy, he that is true, he that hath the key of David, he that openeth and he that shutteth (3:7), my new name

(3:12), the Amen, the faithful and true witness, and the beginning of the creation of God (3:14), Lord God Almighty (4:8), worthy (4:11), the Lion of the tribe of Judah and the Root of David (5:5), a Lamb (5:6), the Lamb that was slain (5:12), Lord holy and true (6:10), him that sitteth on the throne (6:16), the Lamb who is in the midst of the throne (7:17), him that liveth forever and ever and he who created (10:6), our Lord (11:8), his Christ (11:15), her child (12:4), a man child (12:5), the Lamb slain from the foundation of the world (13:8), Jesus (14:12), King of saints (15:3), who art, and wast, and shalt be (16:5), who hath power over these plagues (16:9), God Almighty (16:14), Lord of lords and King of kings (17:14), the Lord God who judgeth her (18:8), the Lord our God (19:1), God that sat on the throne (19:4), Lord God omnipotent (19:6), Faithful and True (19:11), a name written that no man knew (19:12), the Word of God (19:13), Christ (20:4), husband (21:2), God (21:7), the glory of God (21:23), the Lord God of the holy prophets (22:6), the root and offspring of David and the bright and morning star (22:16), he who testifieth these things and Lord Jesus (22:20), our Lord Jesus Christ (22:21).

John was a climactic writer. Like all good writers, he developed his own style. When he wrote, he did so under inspiration and expressed himself climactically. In his Gospel, he builds his case until the reader comes to the climax of the book and falls on his face to declare with Thomas that Jesus is, "My Lord and my God" (John 20:28). Climactically, he wrote the last of the four Gospels. Climactically, he was the last person to write Scripture. Climactically, his Gospel is the greatest thesis on Christ. Climactically, his book was the last to be recognized as canonical. Climactically, he wrote the last book of the Bible. Climactically, he wrote concerning the last things. In baseball, you have to have a finisher, that is, the relief pitcher. If anyone was God's relief pitcher, it was the Apostle John. It should almost be expected that John would be the one chosen of God to give such a full and rich description of Jesus in His names.

This profusion of names and titles, many highly symbolic in meaning in keeping with the nature of the book, provides a composite portrait of the person of Christ. It is truly a "revelation of Jesus Christ" in His names. It is perhaps the fullest description in the New Testament of the majesty of His Being.

Obviously, within the space limitations of this chapter we cannot study all seventy-two names of Jesus in the final book of the Bible. What we shall do, however, is to examine several groups or principal names of Christ in this book. An examination of these names makes us increasingly aware that Jesus can meet any and every need we might have.

JESUS CHRIST

In his brief introduction to the book, John first uses the name "Jesus Christ" (1:1). This is a composite of the personal and official names of Jesus. By the end of the first century, this had become a common way to refer to the Lord. In a sense, it represented a synthesization of the New Testament. Jesus is the predominant name in the Gospels and Acts, whereas Christ is the predominant name in the Epistles, especially the Pauline epistles. We examined both of these names closely in earlier chapters.

A Threefold Picture Of Jesus Christ

John goes on to describe "Jesus Christ, who is the faithful witness, and the first begotten of the dead, and the prince of the kings of the earth" (1:5). This introduces in this book the three primary ideas concerning who Christ is. It is typical throughout the writings of John that although he writes in Greek,

131

he thinks in Hebrew. It is not, therefore, surprising that the Revelation should focus on the threefold Messianic office of prophet, priest, and king.

Jesus Christ is, first, the prophet, and John identifies Him so as "the faithful witness." Jesus came to reveal the Father to mankind and did so perfectly (cf. Matthew 11:27). The Greek word translated "witness" here is *martus,* from which we get the English term "martyr." Originally, *martus* meant "a witness" but came to refer to one who died because of his faithfulness in witnessing. It is interesting to note that Jesus Himself later applied this title to a believer in Pergamum named Antipas (Revelation 2:13). The implication is that just as Jesus is the faithful witness of the Father to us, so we need to be faithful witnesses of Him to the world. This title must have been very meaningful to John, who was himself exiled on Patmos because of his faithful witness of the things of God.

The second of these three titles in Revelation 1:5 emphasizes Christ's role as a priest; He is "the first begotten of the dead." In the Epistle to the Hebrews, He who arose became the high priest. Jesus was the first to rise to eternal life. Others had been raised before but later died again. Theologians call these "resuscitations" as opposed to "resurrections." Also unique concerning the resurrection of Jesus is the fact that He was raised not only to live forever but also to become "a quickening [or life-giving] spirit" (I Corinthians 15:45; Colossians 1:18).

Thirdly, Revelation 1:5 calls Jesus "the prince of the kings of the earth." Although not denying the sovereignty of Christ now as the authority by which kings rule (Romans 13:1) and the "Lord of all" (Acts 10:36), this book emphasizes His coming dominion upon this earth. In this sense, it is right for John to refer to Jesus not only as "king" but also as "prince." A man is a prince until he formally assumes office as king. The next monarch of the British Commonwealth is scheduled to be Prince Charles. Even though he is trained to be king and will someday assume the throne of his mother, until Queen Elizabeth dies or surrenders the throne to her son, Charles will remain a prince. At the beginning of the book of Revelation, Jesus is called a prince of kings, but when He comes to establish His kingdom on earth, He is called "KING OF KINGS, AND LORD OF LORDS" (19:16).

HIS ETERNAL COMPLETENESS AND SUFFICIENCY

Another significant grouping of names appears in Revelation 1:8. The first of these four titles is the "Alpha and Omega." This is the Greek expression of a Hebrew idiom that implies completeness. The Jews took the first and last letters of their alphabet to emphasize and express the entirety of a thing. Alpha is the first letter of the Greek alphabet; omega is the last. A similar English expression is "everything from A to Z." In a sense, this title includes all of the more than 700 names and titles of Jesus (see Appendix where the names and titles of Jesus are listed alphabetically).

In the second of this grouping of names, Jesus is identified as "the beginning and the ending." He is the One who not only pioneers or initiates but also perfects or finishes (cf. Hebrews 12:2). This title serves to emphasize the absolute sovereignty of Christ over history. He is the Lord of history, its beginning, its ending, and all that lies between. Although He may not yet be sitting on the throne of David in Jerusalem, nevertheless, Jesus has control and a unique way of working through others, even using tyrants and terrorists at times to accomplish His purpose (cf. Romans 8:28).

Thirdly, Revelation 1:8 describes Him as "the Lord, which is, and which was, and which is to come." There could be no more specific statement of the deity and eternality of Christ. This title of Christ parallels Moses' great affirmation of faith, "From everlasting to everlasting, thou art God" (Psalm 90:2). Jesus is eternally contemporary, the "I am" of all times. The writer of the Hebrews speaks of "Jesus Christ the same yesterday, and today, and for ever" (Hebrews 13:8).

Finally, Jesus here calls himself "the Almighty." This title probably was not intended to emphasize the omnipotence of Christ, although that attribute of God is certainly implied. Possibly John was thinking in the context of *El Shaddai,* an Old Testament title of God usually translated "God Almighty." Are you trusting the Almighty with your problems in life?

THE SON OF MAN

More than any other book in the New Testament, the book of Revelation draws from the Old Testament, particularly from the Messianic prophecies of the Old Testament. Much of the first three chapters of the Revelation describes a vision of the resurrected and glorified Jesus and His message to seven churches. In this context, John uses many names and titles, but now John introduces Him as "one like unto the Son of man" (1:13). Most conservative commentators agree that this is a reference to the One Daniel called "the Son of man" (Daniel 7:13), who received "dominion, and glory, and a kingdom" from the Ancient of Days (verse 14).

When John turned to see the voice that spoke to him, the first things he observed were seven golden candlesticks. These candlesticks were probably not the kind which decorate homes but, rather, the candlesticks used in Jewish worship. They stood about five feet, five inches tall and weighed about one hundred ten pounds each. They branched out on top to hold several candles; thus, many lights produced the one light of the candlestick. Jesus explains that these candlesticks represent seven local churches in Asia (1:20). It is interesting to note that Jesus was "in the midst of the seven candlesticks—that is, an equal distance from each of them. He was as close to the church in delinquency as He was to the church in revival. Why? Because the whole church is His body.

John pictured Jesus Christ here in the garment of the priest. The vivid description of Christ, as He stood glorified and transfigured before the apostle, tends to emphasize His role as a judge. His head and hair were "white like wool, as white as snow" (1:14), a symbol of His purity. "His eyes were as a flame of fire" (1:14)—that is, they burned through the one whom they saw to discern accurately the nature of man. His feet were compared to "fine brass, as if they burned in a furnace" (1:15). Throughout the Scripture, brass, or more correctly bronze, is offered as a symbol of judgment. His voice is here compared to "the sound of many waters" (1:15), emphasizing His authority. "Out of his mouth went a sharp two-edged sword" (1:16), a symbol of the Word of God in its discerning power (cf. Hebrews 4:12). There was a brilliance about his entire countenance "as the sun shineth in his strength" (1:16).

There in the presence of the glorified, transfigured Christ John fell prostrate to the ground. Like the Old Testament prophets, John was learning experientially that if you really want to do something for God, it begins in the presence of Jesus Christ. Greatness always begins in the presence of God, not at a seminary or Bible college.

This vision of Christ was significant in every detail—from the seven epistles from Jesus to the seven churches in chapters two and three. Each name Jesus used to identify Himself represented His ability to meet the particular need of each church. As we have studied the names of Jesus together, I trust you too have already discovered that whatever your need today, Jesus can meet that need.

The first of the seven churches which Christ addressed was the church at Ephesus. This was a commendable church in many respects, but it had begun to wander from its first love. The church needed leadership which would boldly direct the church back to the place from which they had fallen. To that church,

Jesus identified Himself as "He that holdeth the seven stars in his right hand" (2:1). Earlier John had been told that the stars were the angels or messengers—that is, the pastors of the churches (Revelation 1:20). The senior pastor of the church at Ephesus needed to be encouraged that he was in the right hand of the Saviour as he undertook to lead the flock in that city.

The church at Smyrna was a congregation under intense persecution. Many of their members had already lost their lives because of their faithfulness, and many more would do so in the days to come. They are not criticized in any way by the Lord, only encouraged to remain faithful. To encourage this church, Jesus reminded them He was "the first and the last, which was dead, and is alive" (2:8).

Unlike the above churches, the church at Pergamum (or Pergamos) was a congregation with a mixed multitude. Some of its members gave no evidence of being saved and committed to the Lord. They were somewhat lax in their standards of personal separation and engaged in activities most of the Christians of that day considered wrong. It was a church that was bending to social pressure to conform to the standard of the world and as a result had begun wandering away from their commitment to Biblical authority. More than anything else, the church needed a "back-to-the-Bible revival." To this church, Jesus revealed Himself as "he who hath the sharp sword with two edges" (2:12)—that is, the Word of God.

The church at Thyatira was one which would probably have been rejected as a legitimate church by most evangelical definitions today. A prominent woman in the church was introducing several pagan practices into the church, including immorality and idolatry. Of these two named sins, Jesus appears to be most concerned with her refusal to repent of fornication. As a result, He introduced Himself to that church as the Son of God coming in judgment with His burning eyes and bronze feet (2:18).

The next church Jesus addressed was the church at Sardis.

It was a very reputable church, but in many respects its reputation was all it had. Some commentators identify this church with the Reformation movement in the seventeenth century. The church is described as dead but still possessing a believing remnant. In many respects, although the Reformers helped the church greatly with their reemphasis upon the doctrines of grace, they failed to be as effective as they could be because they neglected the work of the Holy Spirit. Significantly, Jesus reminded this church that it was "he that hath the seven Spirits of God" who addressed them (3:1).

In many respects, the church at Philadelphia enjoyed the most coveted of circumstances among the seven Asian churches. Again, there is nothing Jesus chose to criticize directly. Although the church was small, it had unprecedented opportunities for service ahead of it. It was a church in the midst of revival and simply needed to be reminded not to allow the revival to degenerate into an emotional fanaticism. To this church He identified Himself as "he that is holy, he that is true, he that hath the key of David" (3:7). The reference to "the key of David" originates in Isaiah 22:22 and emphasizes that Christ alone has authority to admit whom He wishes into the kingdom. This church needed truth and holiness, but it also needed to grasp the opportunities that awaited them in reaching their world with the gospel.

The church of Laodicea has come to represent the lukewarm compromise often characteristic of many churches today. They needed to be reminded who Jesus was as "the Amen, the faithful and true witness, the beginning of the creation of God" (3:14). He was to this church the final word, an example that one could be both faithful and true, and a reminder that, as Creator, He knew what was best for His church in Laodicea.

THE LION AND THE LAMB

One of the most interesting contrasts of names in Revelation occurs in chapter five, where in the same context Christ is called both "the Lion of the tribe of Juda" and "a Lamb" (5:5-6). If this combination sounds paradoxical in English, it is even more so in Greek. The word used here for "lamb" is a diminutive and a term of endearment. It is the sort of word a child might use to describe a cute and cuddly baby lamb. And yet, this title is used here in the context of the regal majesty of the Lion of the tribe of Judah, the ruling tribe of Israel.

John here brings together two titles with different emphases to give his readers a fuller understanding of who Jesus is. As the Lion, He is everything the Jews expected in their Messiah. He was the son of David who would rule over Caesar. He was the One coming to establish the kingdom of God on earth. But He was also the Messiah who came to give His life a ransom for many. As such, He is the sacrificial yearling lamb. But He is a lamb with a difference: this lamb had seven horns. A horn was a symbol of power in the Old Testament, and seven was a number of completeness in Scripture. This is the lamb with the fullness of the strength and power of the lion.

When Samson sought to give the Philistines a riddle they could not resolve on their own, he said, "Out of the strong came forth sweetness" (Judges 14:14). Even today, it is uncommon to find strength and sweetness or beauty in the same thing or being. But Jesus manifested both strength and beauty. As we survey the many names and titles of Christ, we note some which emphasize His strength at the same time that others tend to emphasize His gentleness. This is evident in Revelation which emphasizes the fact that God still sits on the throne and will ultimately triumph over the world system: yet, twenty-six times we learn that this God is Jesus the Lamb. The predominant name of Jesus in Revelation is "the lamb."

THE COMING CONQUEROR

The plot of the book of Revelation, particularly from chapter

138

four to the end, views Jesus as the legitimate One to possess the title-deed of the world and notes the preparations in Heaven and events on earth which are necessary for Jesus to claim what is rightfully His and to establish His kingdom. This plot reaches a climax in chapter nineteen, where the second coming of Christ in glory is described. In that passage, Christ is identified by five significant names (19:11-16).

The first of these conquering names of Christ is "Faithful and True" (19:11). Faith/faithfulness and truth are constant themes in the writings of John, Jesus has been identified by these names earlier in Revelation, but for emphasis the compound name appears here at the climax. Right to the end, Jesus is faithful. Right to the end, Jesus is true. This is a tremendous encouragement in time of trial and in those hours when even the finest of Christians begin to wonder, "Is it really worth all this?" Regardless of our circumstances, regardless of our situation, and regardless of how long our circumstances and situation have been like this, Jesus will prove Himself to be faithful and true right to the end.

The second name John records in this passage is "a name written, that no man knew, but he himself" (19:12). This may be one of the most fascinating of all the names of Jesus. Several years ago I became interested in discovering the names of Jesus in Scripture. Originally, I compiled a listing of about 250 names and thought I had exhausted the topic. Yet, as I continued to read and study the Scripture, I came across names that were not on my list. I had heard someone once say that there were 365 names of Christ, one for each day of the year, and wondered whether that was so. To date, I have found over 700 names of Christ, and I am no longer convinced that even this longer list is exhaustive. Each time I discover a new name, I am impressed again by another attribute or aspect of the work of Christ which a name suggests.

139

THE NAMES OF JESUS

As much as I want to know all the names of Jesus, I realize that even at the return of Christ there will be an element of mystery about at least one of His names. When we consider all that is involved in each of the names I have listed in the appendix of this book, it is clear there is no limit to all Jesus is in regard to His names. It would be futile even to try to speculate as to the particular significance of this unknown name in Revelation 19:12. Its presence in Scripture reminds us again that Jesus has a name for every need, even if we don't know the name specifically.

Thirdly, Jesus is called "The Word of God" (19:13). He is the idea or expression of God Himself. This is also one of the birth names of Jesus, and I have dealt more fully with the significance of the *logos* in my chapter on birth names. A fourth name mentioned in this passage is "Almighty God" (19:15), which may refer to *El Shaddai* or, in this context, the omnipotence of God which is an attribute of Jesus.

Finally, John notes the published name embroidered into His garment, "KING OF KINGS, AND LORD OF LORDS" (19:16). With this title He comes, followed by the armies of heaven, which may be an angelic host or more probably the raptured saints. Although I am not much of a rider on horseback today, I hope someday to ride in that heavenly cavalry behind the King of kings and Lord of lords. This title of Christ emphasizes the absolute sovereignty of Jesus.

THE ROOT AND OFFSPRING OF DAVID

In the closing verses of this book, Jesus identifies Himself as "the root and offspring of David" (22:16). This name suggests two ideas in Christ's relationship with David. The first is that of an old root buried in the ground, which from time to time sends up shoots or "suckers" as they are sometimes called. The sucker draws all its strength and nourishment from the root. Those in charge of orchards are continually watching for these new shoots and pruning them back so that the original fruit tree is not robbed of any nourishment the root might otherwise supply to it. Jesus was David's source of strength and nourishment, just as a root supplies the shoot with its strength and nourishment. What was true in David's experience with Christ is also true in the experience of believers today: We derive everything we need from Christ.

But Jesus was not only the source of David but also the seed of David. As the offspring of David, He was the legitimate heir to the throne of his father David. He was the qualified candidate in which all the Messianic prophecies concerning David's greater Son were or shall be fulfilled. He was the Son of David and also David's Lord (Mark 12:35-37). This title was rich in Jewish heritage, for David was considered the model king of Israel.

THE BRIGHT AND MORNING STAR

Again, in identifying another title of Jesus, the Scriptures refer to an image of light. Jesus calls Himself "the bright and morning star" (22:16). This star is so named because it appears on the horizon just before sunrise. The appearance of the morning star tells us that the "dayspring from on high" is almost here. It is the star of hope for those who are tired of the long night of darkness. And with the Apostle John, we are encouraged by this star to pray, "Even so, come, Lord Jesus" (22:20).

CONCLUSION

If Jesus were to come to you today and ask, "What could I do for you?" how would you respond? Actually, the question is not hypothetical. He is here and asking. He wants to become more meaningful in your life by revealing Himself in His names to you. I trust you have learned something new about the Lord Jesus Christ in this brief study of His names, but I

141

hope even more that your new knowledge of Jesus goes beyond the intellect. The names and titles of Jesus in Scripture become ever clearer in the context of your experience with the Lord. Don't be the barrier that prevents Jesus from doing for you what He wants to do in order to make His names a meaningful part of your Christian experience.

For Discussion:

1. Why does the last book in the Bible, Revelation, have perhaps more names of Jesus than any other? What is the main theme of this book?
2. Why is Revelation called a climactic book?
3. What is the threefold picture of Jesus in Revelation? Relate it to His threefold anointed offices.
4. Note the contrasting descriptions of Christ as a Lion and Lamb. How do these titles carry out the theme of Revelation? What do these titles tell us about Christ?
5. Name the titles in Revelation that describe Christ as a conqueror. What do these titles tell us about Christ?
6. Explain how Christ is the Root and Offspring of David.
7. Share briefly something new you have learned about the Lord Jesus Christ in this study of His names.

APPENDIX

The Names and Titles of Jesus Christ in Scripture

THE NAMES AND TITLES OF JESUS CHRIST IN SCRIPTURE

A - 21

The Advocate with the Father (I John 2:1)
Aijeleth Shahar (Psalm 22:Title)
An Alien unto My Mother's Children (Psalm 69:8)
Alive for Evermore (Revelation 1:18)
The All, and in All (Colossians 3:11)
The Almighty Which Is (Revelation 1:8)
The Alpha and Omega (Revelation 1:8)
An Altar (Hebrews 13:10)
The Altogether Lovely (Song of Solomon 5:16)
The Amen (Revelation 3:14)
The Angel of the Covenant (Malachi 3:1)
The Angel of God (Genesis 21:17)
The Angel of His Presence (Isaiah 63:9)
The Angel of the Lord (Genesis 16:7)
The Anointed of God (I Samuel 2:35; Psalm 2:2)
Another King (Acts 17:7)
The Apostle of Our Profession (Hebrews 3:1)
The Ark of the Covenant (Joshua 3:3)
The Arm of the Lord (Isaiah 53:1)
The Author of Eternal Salvation (Hebrews 5:9)
The Author of Our Faith (Hebrews 12:2)

B - 32

The Babe of Bethlehem (Luke 2:12, 16)
The Balm in Gilead (Jeremiah 8:22)
A Banner to Them that Fear Thee (Psalm 60:4)
The Bearer of Glory (Zechariah 6:13)
The Bearer of Sin (Hebrews 9:28)

The Beauties of Holiness (Psalm 110:3)
Before All Things (Colossians 1:17)
The Beginning (Colossians 1:18)
The Beginning of the Creation of God (Revelation 3:14)
The Beginning and the Ending (Revelation 1:8)
The Beloved (Ephesians 1:6)
My Beloved Son (Matthew 3:17)
The Better (Hebrews 7:7)
The Bishop of Your Souls (I Peter 2:25)
The Blessed and Only Potentate (I Timothy 6:15)
The Blessed for Evermore (II Corinthians 11:31)
The Blessed Hope (Titus 2:13)
The Branch (Zechariah 3:8; 6:12)
The Branch of the Lord (Isaiah 4:2)
The Branch of Righteousness (Jeremiah 33:15)
The Branch Out of His Roots (Isaiah 11:1)
The Bread of God (John 6:33)
The Bread of Life (John 6:35)
The Breaker (Micah 2:13)
The Bridegroom of the Bride (John 3:29)
The Bright and Morning Star (Revelation 22:16)
The Brightness of His Glory (Hebrews 1:3)
The Brightness of Thy Rising (Isaiah 60:3)
Our Brother (Matthew 12:50)
A Buckler (Psalm 18:30)
The Builder of the Temple (Zechariah 6:12-13)
A Bundle of Myrrh (Song of Solomon 1:13)

C - 40

The Captain of the Hosts of the Lord (Joshua 5:14-15)
The Captain of Their Salvation (Hebrews 2:10)
The Carpenter (Mark 6:3)

THE NAMES OF JESUS

The Carpenter's Son (Matthew 13:55)
A Certain Nobleman (Luke 19:12)
A Certain Samaritan (Luke 10:33)
The Chief Cornerstone (Ephesians 2:20; I Peter 2:6)
The Chief Shepherd (I Peter 5:4)
The Chiefest Among Ten Thousand (Song of Solomon 5:10)
A Child Born (Isaiah 9:6)
Child of the Holy Ghost (Matthew 1:18)
The Child Jesus (Luke 2:27, 43)
The Chosen of God (I Peter 2:4)
Chosen out of the People (Psalm 89:19)
Christ (Matthew 1:16)
The Christ (I John 5:1)
Christ Come in the Flesh (I John 4:2)
Christ Crucified (I Corinthians 1:23)
The Christ of God (Luke 9:20)
Christ Jesus (Acts 19:4)
Christ Jesus the Lord (II Corinthians 4:5)
Christ a King (Luke 23:2)
Christ the Lord (Luke 2:11)
Christ Our Passover (I Corinthians 5:7)
Christ Risen from the Dead (I Corinthians 15:20)
The Chosen of God (Luke 23:35)
A Cleft of the Rock (Exodus 33:22)
A Cluster of Camphire (Song of Solomon 1:14)
The Comforter (John 14:16-18)
A Commander to the Peoples (Isaiah 55:4)
Conceived of the Holy Spirit (Matthew 1:20)
The Consolation of Israel (Luke 2:25)
The Corn of Wheat (John 12:24)
Counselor (Isaiah 9:6)
The Covenant of the People (Isaiah 42:6; 49:8)
The Covert from the Tempest (Isaiah 32:2)
The Covert of Thy Wings (Psalm 61:4)

The Creator (Romans 1:25)
The Creator of the Ends of the Earth (Isaiah 40:28)
A Crown of Glory (Isaiah 28:5)

D - 17

My Darling (Psalm 22:20)
David (Matthew 1:17)
The Day (II Peter 1:19)
The Daysman Betwixt Us (Job 9:33)
The Dayspring from on High (Luke 1:78)
The Daystar to Arise (II Peter 1:19)
His Dear Son (Colossians 1:13)
That Deceiver (Matthew 27:63)
My Defense (Psalm 94:22)
The Deliverance of Zion (Joel 2:32)
My Deliverer (Psalm 40:17)
The Desire of All Nations (Haggai 2:7)
Despised by the People (Psalm 22:6)
The Dew of Israel (Hosea 14:5)
A Diadem of Beauty (Isaiah 28:5)
The Door of the Sheep (John 10:7)
Dwelling Place (Psalm 90:1)

E - 17

Mine Elect (Isaiah 42:1)
Eliakim (Isaiah 22:20)
Elijah (Matthew 16:14)
Emmanuel (Matthew 1:23)
The End of the Law (Romans 10:4)
The Ensign of the People (Isaiah 11:10)
Equal with God (Philippians 2:6)
The Eternal God (Deuteronomy 33:27)
That Eternal Life (I John 1:2)

THE NAMES OF JESUS

The Everlasting Father (Isaiah 9:6)
An Everlasting Light (Isaiah 60:19,20)
An Everlasting Name (Isaiah 63:12)
Thy Exceedingly Great Reward (Genesis 15:1)
His Excellency (Job 13:11)
The Excellency of Our God (Isaiah 35:2)
Excellent (Psalm 8:1,9)
The Express Image of His Person (Hebrews 1:3)

F - 38

The Face of the Lord (Luke 1:76)
The Fairer than the Children of Men (Psalm 45:2)
Faithful (I Thessalonians 5:24)
Faithful and True (Revelation 19:11)
The Faithful and True Witness (Revelation 3:14)
A Faithful Creator (I Peter 4:19)
A Faithful High Priest (Hebrews 2:17)
A Faithful Priest (I Samuel 2:35)
The Faithful Witness (Revelation 1:5)
A Faithful Witness Between Us (Jeremiah 42:5)
A Faithful Witness in Heaven (Psalm 89:37)
My Father (Psalm 89:26)
A Father of the Fatherless (Psalm 68:5)
The Feast (I Corinthians 5:8)
My Fellow (Zechariah 13:7)
The Finisher of the Faith (Hebrews 12:2)
The First and the Last (Revelation 1:8)
The First Begotten (Hebrews 1:6)
The Firstborn (Hebrews 12:23)
The Firstborn among Many Brethren (Romans 8:29)
The Firstborn of the Dead (Revelation 1:5—KJV "begotten")
The Firstborn of Every Creature (Colossians 1:15)

150

Her Firstborn Son (Luke 2:7)
The First Fruit (Romans 11:16)
The Firstfruits of Them That Sleep (I Corinthians 15:20)
Flesh (John 1:14)
The Foolishness of God (I Corinthians 1:25)
Foreordained before the Foundation of the World (I Peter 1:20)
The Forerunner (Hebrews 6:20)
Fortress (Psalm 18:2)
The Foundation Which Is Laid (I Corinthians 3:11)
The Fountain of Life (Psalm 36:9)
The Fountain of Living Waters (Jeremiah 17:13)
The Free Gift (Romans 5:15)
The Friend of Publicans and Sinners (Matthew 11:9; Luke 7:34)
A Friend that Sticketh Closer than a Brother (Proverbs 18:24)
The Fruit of the Earth (Isaiah 4:2)
The Fruit of Thy Womb (Luke 1:42)
Fullers' Soap (Malachi 3:2)

G - 47

The Gift of God (John 4:10)
A Gin (Isaiah 8:14)
A Glorious High Throne from the Beginning (Jeremiah 17:12)
A Glorious Name (Isaiah 63:14)
Glory (Haggai 2:7)
My Glory (Psalm 3:3)
The Glory as of the Only Begotten of the Father (John 1:14)
The Glory of God (Romans 3:23)
The Glory of His Father (Matthew 16:27; Mark 8:38)
God (Revelation 21:7)
God Who Avengeth Me (Psalm 18:47)
God Blessed Forever (Romans 9:5)
God Who Forgavest Them (Psalm 99:8)

THE NAMES OF JESUS

Our God Forever and Ever (Psalm 48:14)
The God of Glory (Psalm 29:3)
The God of Israel (Psalm 59:5)
The God of Jacob (Psalm 46:7)
The God of My Life (Psalm 42:8)
The God of My Mercy (Psalm 59:10)
God in the Midst of Her (Psalm 46:5)
God Manifest in the Flesh (I Timothy 3:16)
God of My Righteousness (Psalm 4:1)
God of My Salvation (Psalm 18:46; 24:5)
God of My Strength (Psalm 43:2)
God with Us (Matthew 1:23)
A Good Man (John 7:12)
The Goodman of the House (Matthew 20:11)
Good Master (Matthew 19:16)
The Good Shepherd (John 10:11)
The Governor Among Nations (Psalm 22:28)
Great (Jeremiah 32:18)
The Great God (Titus 2:13)
A Great High Priest (Hebrews 4:14)
A Great Light (Isaiah 9:2)
A Great Prophet (Luke 7:16)
That Great Shepherd of the Sheep (Hebrews 13:20)
Greater (I John 4:4)
A Greater and More Perfect Tabernacle (Hebrews 9:11)
Greater Than Our Father Abraham (John 8:53, 57-58)
Greater Than Our Father Jacob (John 4:12)
Greater Than Jonah (Matthew 12:41)
Greater Than Solomon (Matthew 12:42)
Greater Than the Temple (Matthew 12:6)
Guest (Luke 19:7)
Our Guide Even Unto Death (Psalm 48:14)
The Guide of My Youth (Jeremiah 3:4)
The Guiltless (Matthew 12:7)

H - 41

The Habitation of Justice (Jeremiah 50:7)
Harmless (Hebrews 7:26)
An He Goat (Proverbs 30:31)
The Head of All Principality and Power (Colossians 2:10)
The Head of Every Man (I Corinthians 11:3)
The Head of the Body, the Church (Colossians 1:18)
The Head of the Corner (I Peter 2:7)
The Health of My Countenance (Psalm 42:11)
The Heir (Mark 12:7)
Heir of All Things (Hebrews 1:2)
My Helper (Hebrews 13:6; Psalm 32:7)
The Helper of the Fatherless (Psalm 10:14)
A Hen (Matthew 23:37)
The Hidden Manna (Revelation 2:17)
My Hiding Place (Psalm 32:7)
A Hiding Place from the Wind (Isaiah 32:2)
The High and Lofty One Who Inhabiteth Eternity (Isaiah 57:15)
An High Priest (Hebrews 5:5)
An High Priest after the Order of Melchisedec (Hebrews 5:10)
An High Priest Forever (Hebrews 6:20)
My High Tower (Psalm 18:2)
The Highest Himself (Psalm 87:5)
An Highway (Isaiah 35:8)
Holy (Isaiah 57:15)
Thy Holy Child Jesus (Acts 4:27)
Thine Holy One (Acts 2:27)
The Holy One and Just (Acts 3:14)
The Holy One of Israel (Psalm 89:18)
That Holy Thing Which Shall Be Born of Thee (Luke 1:35)
Holy to the Lord (Luke 2:23)
Our Hope (I Timothy 1:1)
The Hope of Glory (Colossians 1:27)

THE NAMES OF JESUS

The Hope of His People (Joel 3:16)
The Hope of Israel (Acts 28:20)
The Hope of Their Fathers (Jeremiah 50:7)
The Horn of David (Psalm 132:17)
The Horn of the House of Israel (Ezekiel 29:21)
An Horn of Salvation (Luke 1:69)
An House of Defense (Psalm 31:2)
An Householder (Matthew 20:1)
Her Husband (Revelation 21:2)

I - 5

I Am (John 18:6)
The Image of the Invisible God (Colossians 1:15)
Immanuel (Isaiah 7:14)
Innocent Blood (Matthew 27:4)
Isaac (Hebrews 11:17,18)

J - 17

The Jasper Stone (Revelation 4:3)
Jeremiah (Matthew 16:14)
Jesus (Matthew 1:21)
Jesus Christ (Hebrews 13:8)
Jesus Christ the Lord (Romans 7:25)
Jesus Christ, the Son of God (John 20:31)
Jesus of Galilee (Matthew 26:69)
Jesus of Nazareth (John 1:45)
Jesus of Nazareth, the King of the Jews (John 19:19)
A Jew (John 4:9)
John the Baptist (Matthew 16:14)
Joseph's Son (Luke 4:22)
The Judge of All the Earth (Genesis 18:25)
The Judge of the Quick and the Dead (Acts 10:42)

A Judge of the Widows (Psalm 68:5)
The Just One (Acts 7:52)
This Just Person (Matthew 27:24)

K - 22

Thy Keeper (Psalm 121:5)
The Kindness and Love of God (Titus 3:4)
Another King (Acts 17:7)
The King Eternal (I Timothy 1:17)
The King Immortal (I Timothy 1:17)
The King in His Beauty (Isaiah 33:17)
The King Forever and Ever (Psalm 10:16)
The King Invisible (I Timothy 1:17)
The King of All the Earth (Psalm 47:7)
The King of Glory (Psalm 24:7,8)
The King of Heaven (Daniel 4:37)
The King of Israel (John 1:49)
King of Kings (Revelation 19:16)
The King of Peace (Hebrews 7:2)
The King of Righteousness (Hebrews 7:2)
King of Saints (Revelation 15:3)
The King of Salem (Hebrews 7:2)
The King of Terrors (Job 18:14)
King of the Jews (Matthew 2:2)
The King Who Cometh in the Name of the Lord (Luke 19:38)
The King's Son (Psalm 72:1)
The Kinsman (Ruth 4:14)

L - 58

A Ladder (Genesis 28:12)
The Lamb (Revelation 17:14)
The Lamb of God (John 1:29)
The Lamb Slain from the Foundation of the World

(Revelation 13:8)
The Lamb That Was Slain (Revelation 5:12)
The Lamb Who Is in the Midst of the Throne (Revelation 7:17)
The Last (Isaiah 44:6)
The Last Adam (I Corinthians 15:45)
The Lawgiver (James 4:12)
A Leader (Isaiah 55:4)
The Life (John 14:6)
The Lifter-Up of Mine Head (Psalm 3:3)
The Light (John 1:7)
The Light of Men (John 1:4)
The Light of the City (Revelation 21:23)
The Light of the Glorious Gospel of Christ (II Corinthians 4:4)
The Light of the Knowledge of the Glory of God
     (II Corinthians 4:6)
The Light of the Morning (II Samuel 23:4)
The Light of the World (John 8:12)
The Light of Truth (Psalm 43:3)
A Light to Lighten Gentiles (Luke 2:32)
A Light to the Gentiles (Isaiah 49:6)
The Lily among Thorns (Song of Solomon 2:2)
The Lily of the Valleys (Song of Solomon 2:1)
The Lion of the Tribe of Judah (Revelation 5:5)
The Living Bread (John 6:51)
The Living God (Psalm 42:2)
Lord - *despotes* (II Peter 2:1)
Lord - *kurios* (John 13:13)
Lord - *rabboni* (Mark 10:51)
Lord Also of the Sabbath (Mark 2:28)
My Lord and My God (John 20:28)
The Lord and Saviour (II Peter 1:11)
Lord Both of the Dead and Living (Romans 14:9)
The Lord from Heaven (I Corinthians 15:47)
Lord God Almighty (Revelation 16:7)
The Lord God of the Holy Prophets (Revelation 22:6)

Lord God of Israel (Psalm 41:13)
Lord God of Truth (Psalm 31:5)
Lord God Omnipotent (Revelation 19:6)
The Lord God Who Judgeth Her (Revelation 18:8)
The Lord, Holy and True (Revelation 6:10)
Lord Jesus (Romans 10:9)
Lord Jesus Christ (James 2:1)
The Lord Mighty in Battle (Psalm 24:8)
The Lord of All the Earth (Joshua 3:11)
The Lord of Glory (I Corinthians 2:8)
The Lord of the Harvest (Matthew 9:38)
The Lord of Hosts (Psalm 24:10)
O LORD Our Lord (Psalm 8:1,9)
Lord of Lords (I Timothy 6:15)
Lord of Peace (II Thessalonians 3:16)
The Lord of the Vineyard (Matthew 20:8)
The Lord of the Whole Earth (Psalm 97:5)
The Lord's Christ (Revelation 11:15)
The Lord's Doing (Matthew 21:42)
The Lord Strong and Mighty (Psalm 24:8)
Lowly in Heart (Matthew 11:29)

M - 42

Magnified (Psalm 40:16)
Our Maker (Psalm 95:6)
A Malefactor (John 18:30)
The Man (John 19:5)
A Man Approved of God (Acts 2:22)
A Man Child (Revelation 12:5)
The Man Christ Jesus (I Timothy 2:5)
A Man Gluttonous (Matthew 11:19)
The Man Whose Name Is the Branch (Zechariah 6:12)

THE NAMES OF JESUS

The Man of Sorrows (Isaiah 53:3)
The Man Whom He Hath Ordained (Acts 17:31)
Manna (Exodus 16:15)
Marvelous in Our Eyes (Matthew 21:42)
The Master - *didaskalos* (John 11:28)
Master - *epistates* (Luke 5:5)
Your Master - *kathegetes* (Matthew 23:10)
The Master of the House - *oikodespotes* (Luke 13:25)
Master - *rabbi* (John 4:31)
The Meat Offering (Leviticus 2:1)
The Mediator (I Timothy 2:5)
The Mediator of a Better Covenant (Hebrews 8:6)
The Mediator of the New Covenant (Hebrews 12:24)
The Mediator of the New Testament (Hebrews 9:15)
Meek (Matthew 11:29)
Melchizedek (Genesis 14:18)
A Merciful and Faithful High Priest (Hebrews 2:17)
His Mercy and His Truth (Psalm 57:3)
Mercyseat (Hebrews 9:5; I John 2:2)
The Messenger of the Covenant (Malachi 3:1)
Messiah (Daniel 9:26)
Messiah the Prince (Daniel 9:25)
Mighty (Psalm 89:19)
The Mighty God (Isaiah 9:6)
The Mighty One of Jacob (Isaiah 49:26; 60:16)
The Minister of Sin (Galatians 2:17)
A Minister of the Circumcision (Romans 15:8)
The Minister of the Heavenly Sanctuary (Hebrews 8:1-3)
A More Excellent Name (Hebrews 1:4)
The Morning Star (Revelation 2:28)
The Most High (Psalm 9:2; 21:7)
The Mouth of God (Matthew 4:4)
The Mystery of God (Colossians 2:2)

N - 5

A Nail Fastened in a Sure Place (Isaiah 22:23)
A Name above Every Name (Philippians 2:9)
A Nazarene (Matthew 2:23)
Thy New Name (Revelation 3:12)
A Nourisher of Thine Old Age (Ruth 4:15)

O - 9

An Offering and a Sacrifice to God (Ephesians 5:2)
The Offspring of David (Revelation 22:16)
Ointment Poured Forth (Song of Solomon 1:3)
The Omega (Revelation 22:13)
His Only Begotten Son (John 3:16)
The Only Begotten of the Father (John 1:14)
Only Potentate (I Timothy 6:15)
The Only Wise God (I Timothy 1:17)
An Owl of the Desert (Psalm 102:6)

P - 40

Our Passover (I Corinthians 5:7)
The Path of Life (Psalm 16:11)
A Pavilion (Psalm 31:20)
Our Peace (Ephesians 2:14)
The Peace-Offering (Leviticus 3:1)
A Pelican of the Wilderness (Psalm 102:6)
A Perfect Man (James 3:2)
The Person of Christ (II Corinthians 2:10)
Physician (Luke 4:23)
The Pillar of Fire (Exodus 13:21,22)
The Place of Our Sanctuary (Jeremiah 17:12)
A Place of Refuge (Isaiah 4:6)
A Plant of Renown (Ezekiel 34:29)

THE NAMES OF JESUS

A Polished Staff (Isaiah 49:2)
Poor (II Corinthians 8:9)
My Portion (Psalm 119:57)
The Portion of Jacob (Jeremiah 51:19)
The Portion of Mine Inheritance (Psalm 16:5)
The Potter (Jeremiah 18:6)
The Power of God (I Corinthians 1:24)
Precious (I Peter 2:7)
A Precious Cornerstone (Isaiah 28:16)
The Preeminence (Colossians 1:18)
A Price (I Corinthians 6:20)
The Price of His Redemption (Leviticus 25:52)
A Priest Forever (Psalm 110:4)
The Priest of the Most High God (Hebrews 7:1)
A Prince and Saviour (Acts 5:31)
The Prince of Life (Acts 3:15)
The Prince of Peace (Isaiah 9:6)
Prince of Princes (Daniel 8:25)
The Prince of the Kings of the Earth (Revelation 1:5)
The Prophet (John 7:40)
A Prophet Mighty in Deed and Word (Luke 24:19)
The Prophet of Nazareth (Matthew 21:11)
A Prophet without Honor (Matthew 13:57)
One of the Prophets (Matthew 16:14)
The Propitiation for Our Sins (I John 2:2)
Pure (I John 3:3)
A Purifier of Silver (Malachi 3:3)

Q - 2

Of Quick Understanding (Isaiah 11:3)
A Quickening Spirit (I Corinthians 15:45)

R - 53

Rabbi (John 3:2)
Rabboni (John 20:16)
Rain upon the Mown Grass (Psalm 72:6)
A Ransom for All (I Timothy 2:6)
A Ransom for Many (Matthew 20:28)
The Red Heifer without Spot (Numbers 19:2)
My Redeemer (Job 19:25)
Redemption (I Corinthians 1:30; Luke 21:28)
The Redemption of Their Soul (Psalm 49:8)
A Refiner's Fire (Malachi 3:2)
Our Refuge (Psalm 46:1)
A Refuge in Times of Trouble (Psalm 9:9)
A Refuge for the Oppressed (Psalm 9:9)
A Refuge from the Storm (Isaiah 25:4)
Our Report (Isaiah 53:1)
A Reproach of Men (Psalm 22:6)
Their Resting Place (Jeremiah 50:6)
A Restorer of Thy Life (Ruth 4:15)
The Resurrection and the Life (John 11:25)
The Revelation of Jesus Christ (Revelation 1:1)
Reverend (Psalm 111:9)
A Reward for the Righteous (Psalm 58:11)
Rich (Romans 10:12)
The Riches of His Glory (Romans 9:23)
The Riddle (Judges 14:14)
Right (Deuteronomy 32:4)
The Righteous (I John 2:1)
A Righteous Branch (Jeremiah 23:5)
The Righteous God (Psalm 7:9)
The Righteous Lord (Psalm 11:7)
My Righteous Servant (Isaiah 53:11)
The Righteous Judge (II Timothy 4:8)

THE NAMES OF JESUS

A Righteous Man (Luke 23:47)
Righteousness (I Corinthians 1:30)
The Righteousness of God (Romans 10:3)
A River of Water in a Dry Place (Isaiah 32:2)
The Rock (Matthew 16:18)
The Rock that Is Higher Than I (Psalm 61:2)
The Rock of Israel (II Samuel 23:3)
A Rock of Offense (Romans 9:33)
The Rock of My Refuge (Psalm 94:22)
The Rock of His Salvation (Deuteronomy 32:15)
The Rock of Our Salvation (Psalm 95:1)
The Rock of Thy Strength (Isaiah 17:10)
The Rod (Micah 6:9)
A Rod out of the Stem of Jesse (Isaiah 11:1)
The Root of David (Revelation 5:5)
A Root of Jesse (Romans 15:12; Isaiah 11:10)
A Root out of Dry Ground (Isaiah 53:2)
The Root and Offspring of David (Revelation 22:16)
The Rose of Sharon (Song of Solomon 2:1)
A Ruler (Micah 5:2)

S - 94

The Sacrifice for Sins (Hebrews 10:12)
A Sacrifice to God (Ephesians 5:2)
My Salvation (Psalm 27:1)
The Salvation of God (Luke 2:30; 3:6)
The Salvation of Israel (Jeremiah 3:23)
A Samaritan (John 8:48)
The Same Yesterday, Today and Forever (Hebrews 13:8)
A Sanctuary (Isaiah 8:14)
A Sardius Stone (Revelation 4:3)
The Saving Strength of His Anointed (Psalm 28:8)
Saviour (Titus 2:13)

The Saviour of All Men (I Timothy 4:10)
The Saviour of the Body (Ephesians 5:23)
The Saviour of the World (John 4:42; I John 4:14)
The Scapegoat (Leviticus 16:8; John 11:49-52)
The Scepter of Israel (Numbers 24:17)
The Scepter of Thy Kingdom (Psalm 45:6)
The Second Man (I Corinthians 15:45)
Secret (Judges 13:18)
The Secret of Thy Presence (Psalm 31:20)
The Seed of Abraham (Galatians 3:16)
The Seed of David (Romans 1:3; II Timothy 2:8)
The Seed of the Woman (Genesis 3:15)
The Sent One (John 9:4)
Separate from His Brethren (Genesis 49:26)
Separate from Sinners (Hebrews 7:26)
The Serpent in the Wilderness (John 3:14)
My Servant (Isaiah 42:1)
A Servant of Rulers (Isaiah 49:7)
My Servant the Branch (Zechariah 3:8)
A Shadow from the Heat (Isaiah 25:4)
The Shadow of the Almighty (Psalm 91:1)
The Shadow of A Great Rock (Isaiah 32:2)
A Shelter (Psalm 61:3)
My Shepherd (Psalm 23:1; Isaiah 40:11)
Shepherd of Israel (Psalm 80:1)
Our Shield (Psalm 84:9)
Shiloh (Genesis 49:10)
Shoshannim (Psalm 45:Title; 69:Title)
A Sign of the Lord (Isaiah 7:11)
Siloam (John 9:7)
Sin (II Corinthians 5:21)
A Snare to the Inhabitants of Jerusalem (Isaiah 8:14)
The Son (Matthew 11:27)
His Son from Heaven (I Thessalonians 1:10)

THE NAMES OF JESUS

A Son Given (Isaiah 9:6)
The Son of Abraham (Matthew 1:1)
The Son of David (Matthew 1:1)
The Son of God (John 1:49)
The Son of Joseph (John 1:45)
The Son of Man (John 1:51)
The Son of Mary (Mark 6:3)
The Son of the Blessed (Mark 14:61)
The Son of the Father (II John 3)
The Son of the Freewoman (Galatians 4:30)
The Son of the Highest (Luke 1:32)
The Son of the Living God (Matthew 16:16)
The Son of the Most High (Mark 5:7)
A Son over His Own House (Hebrews 3:6)
The Son Who Is Consecrated for Evermore (Hebrews 7:28)
My Song (Isaiah 12:2)
A Sower (Matthew 13:4,37)
A Sparrow Alone upon the Housetop (Psalm 102:7)
That Spiritual Rock (I Corinthians 10:4)
A Star out of Jacob (Numbers 24:17)
My Stay (Psalm 18:18)
A Stone Cut out of the Mountain (Daniel 2:45)
A Stone Cut without Hands (Daniel 2:34)
The Stone of Israel (Genesis 49:24)
A Stone of Stumbling (I Peter 2:8)
The Stone Which the Builders Refused (Psalm 118:22)
The Stone Which the Builders Rejected (Matthew 21:42)
The Stone Which Was Set at Nought (Acts 4:11)
A Stranger (Matthew 25:35)
My Strength (Isaiah 12:2)
The Strength of Israel (I Samuel 15:29)
The Strength of My Life (Psalm 27:1)
A Strength to the Needy in Distress (Isaiah 25:4)
A Strength to the Poor (Isaiah 25:4)
Strong (Psalm 24:8)

A Strong Consolation (Hebrews 6:18)
A Stronghold in the Day of Trouble (Nahum 1:7)
A Strong Lord (Psalm 89:8)
My Strong Refuge (Psalm 71:7)
My Strong Rock (Psalm 31:2)
A Strong Tower (Proverbs 18:10)
A Strong Tower from the Enemy (Psalm 61:3)
A Stronger than He (Luke 11:22)
A Stumbling Block (I Corinthians 1:23)
The Sun of Righteousness (Malachi 4:2)
A Sure Foundation (Isaiah 28:16)
The Sure Mercies of David (Isaiah 55:3; Acts 13:34)
A Surety of A Better Testament (Hebrews 7:22)
A Sweet-Smelling Savor (Ephesians 5:2)

T - 19

A Tabernacle for a Shadow (Isaiah 4:6)
The Tabernacle of God (Revelation 21:3)
Teacher (Matthew 10:25)
A Teacher Come from God (John 3:2)
The Temple (John 2:19)
The Tender Grass (II Samuel 23:4)
A Tender Plant (Isaiah 53:2)
The Tender Mercy of God (Luke 1:78)
The Testator (Hebrews 9:16,17)
The Testimony of God (I Corinthians 2:1)
This Treasure (II Corinthians 4:7)
The Trespass Offering (Leviticus 5:6)
A Tried Stone (Isaiah 28:16)
The True Bread from Heaven (John 6:32)
The True God (Jeremiah 10:10)
The True Light (John 1:9)
The True Vine (John 15:1)

THE NAMES OF JESUS

The True Witness (Proverbs 14:25)
The Truth (John 14:6)

U - 7

Undefiled (Hebrews 7:26)
Understanding (Proverbs 3:19)
The Unknown God (Acts 17:23)
The Unspeakable Gift (II Corinthians 9:15)
The Urim and Thummin (Exodus 28:30)
The Upholder of All Things (Hebrews 1:3)
Upright (Psalm 92:15)

V - 7

The Veil (Hebrews 10:20)
The Very God of Peace (I Thessalonians 5:23)
Very Great (Psalm 104:1)
A Very Present Help in Trouble (Psalm 46:1)
The Victory (I Corinthians 15:54)
The Vine (John 15:5)
The Voice (Revelation 1:12)

W - 24

A Wall of Fire (Zechariah 2:5)
The Wave-Offering (Leviticus 7:30)
The Way (John 14:6)
The Way of Holiness (Isaiah 35:8)
The Weakness of God (I Corinthians 1:25)
A Wedding Garment (Matthew 22:12)
The Well of Living Waters (John 4:14)
The Well of Salvation (Isaiah 12:3)
Wisdom (I Corinthians 1:25)

The Wisdom of God (I Corinthians 1:24)
A Wise Master Builder (I Corinthians 3:10)
Witness (Judges 11:10)
My Witness (Job 16:19)
The Witness of God (I John 5:9)
A Witness to the People (Isaiah 55:4)
Wonderful (Judges 13:18)
Wonderful Counselor (Isaiah 9:6)
The Word (John 1:1)
The Word of God (Revelation 19:13)
The Word of Life (I John 1:1)
A Worm and No Man (Psalm 22:6)
Worthy (Revelation 4:11; 5:12)
That Worthy Name (James 2:7)
Worthy to be Praised (Psalm 18:3)

X - 2

X as *Chi* The Traditional Symbol of Christ
X as an Unknown Quantity (Revelation 19:12)

Y - 2

The Yokefellow (Matthew 11:29-30)
The Young Child (Matthew 2:11)

Z - 4

Zaphnath-paaneah (Genesis 41:45)
The Zeal of the Lord of Hosts (Isaiah 37:32)
The Zeal of Thine House (John 2:17; Psalm 69:9)
Zerubbabel (Zechariah 4:7,9)

Total Names and Titles - 675

THE PREEMINENT PRONOUNS OF CHRIST
IN SCRIPTURE

Who Art, and Wast, and Shalt Be (Revelation 16:5)
Him That Bringeth Good Tidings (Nahum 1:15)
He Who Brought Us Up (Joshua 24:17)
He Who Created (Revelation 10:6)
He That Cometh (Luke 7:19; Matthew 11:14)
He That Cometh after Me (John 1:15, 27)
He Who Cometh down from Heaven (John 6:33)
He That Cometh in the Name of the Lord (Matthew 21:9)
He That Cometh into the World (John 11:27)
Who Coverest Thyself with Light (Psalm 104:2)
Who Crowneth Thee with Loving-Kindness (Psalm 103:4)
He That was Dead and Is Alive (Revelation 2:8)
Who Dwelleth in Zion (Psalm 9:11)
He Who Fighteth for You (Joshua 23:10)
He That Filleth All in All (Ephesians 1:23)
Who Forgiveth All Thine Iniquities (Psalm 103:3)
This That Forgiveth Sins (Luke 7:49)
Who Girdeth Me with Strength (Psalm 18:32)
Who Giveth Me Counsel (Psalm 16:7)
He That Hath the Bride (John 3:29)
He Who Hath His Eyes Like a Flame of Fire
    (Revelation 2:18)
He Who Hath His Feet Like Fine Brass
    (Revelation 2:18)
Thou Who Hearest Prayer (Psalm 65:2)
Who Healeth all Thy Diseases (Psalm 103:3)
He That Is Higher Than the Highest (Ecclesiastes 5:8)
He That Holdeth the Seven Stars (Revelation 2:1)
He That Is Holy (Revelation 3:7)
He That Keepeth Israel (Psalm 121:4)

He That Hath the Key of David (Revelation 3:7)
Who Laid the Foundations of the Earth (Psalm 104:5)
Who Layeth the Beams of His Chambers in the Waters
    (Psalm 104:3)
Thou Who Liftest Me up from the Gates of Death
    (Psalm 9:13)
He That Liveth (Revelation 1:18)
Him That Liveth Forever and Ever (Revelation 10:6)
Him That Loveth Us (Revelation 1:5)
Who Maketh His Angels Spirits (Psalm 104:4; Hebrews 1:7)
Who Maketh the Clouds His Chariot (Psalm 104:3)
He That Openeth (Revelation 3:7)
Who Hast Power over These Plagues (Revelation 16:9)
Who Redeemeth Thy Life from Destruction (Psalm 103:4)
Thou Rulest the Raging of the Sea (Psalm 89:9)
He That Sanctifieth (Hebrews 2:11)
Who Satisfieth Thy Mouth with Good Things (Psalm 103:5)
Thou Who Saveth by Thy Right Hand (Psalm 17:7)
Who Saveth the Upright in Heart (Psalm 7:10)
He Who Searcheth (Revelation 2:23)
Whom Thou hast Sent (John 17:3)
He Who Hath the Seven Spirits of God (Revelation 3:1)
He Who Hath the Sharp Sword with Two Edges
    (Revelation 2:12)
He that Shutteth (Revelation 3:7)
He Who Sitteth in the Heavens (Psalm 2:4)
Him That Sitteth on the Throne (Revelation 6:16)
Who Stretchest out the Heavens Like a Curtain
    (Psalm 104:2)
He Who Testifieth (Revelation 22:20)
He That Is True (Revelation 3:7)
Him That Was Valued (Matthew 27:9)
He Who Walketh in the Midst of the Seven Candlesticks
    (Revelation 2:1)

Who Walketh upon the Wings of the Wind (Psalm 104:3)

Total - 58

THE COMPOUND NAMES OF THE LORD GOD
(JEHOVAH EL) IN SCRIPTURE

El Elohim Jehovah - The Lord God of gods (Joshua 22:22)

Jehovah Elohim - The Lord God (Genesis 2:4; 3:9-13,21)

Jehovah Elohe 'Abothekem - The Lord God of Your Fathers (Joshua 18:3)

Jehovah El Elyon - The Lord, the Most High God (Genesis 14:22)

Jehovah El 'Emeth - The Lord God of Truth (Psalm 31:5)

Jehovah El Gemuwal - The Lord God of Recompense (Jeremiah 51:56)

Jehovah Elohim Tseba'oth - The Lord God of Hosts (Psalm 59:5)

Jehovah Elohe Yeshu'athi - The Lord God of my Salvation (Psalm 88:1)

Jehovah Elohe Yisra'el - The Lord God of Israel (Psalm 41:13)

Total - 9

THE NAME OF GOD (ELOHIM) IN SCRIPTURE

Elohim - God (Genesis 1:1)

Elohim Bashamayim - God in Heaven (Joshua 2:11)

El Bethel - The God of the House of God (Genesis 35:7)

Elohe Chaseddiy - God of My Mercy (Psalm 59:10)

El Elohe Yisra'el - God, the God of Israel (Genesis 33:20; Psalm 68:8)

El Elyon - The Most High God (Genesis 14:18)

El Emunah - A Faithful God (Deuteronomy 7:9)

El Gibbor - The Mighty God (Isaiah 9:6)

El Hakabodh - The God of Glory (Psalm 29:3)

El Hayyay - God of My Life (Psalm 42:8)

El He - The Living God (Joshua 3:10)

El Kana - A Jealous God (Exodus 20:5)

Elohim Kedoshim - A Holy God (Joshua 24:19)

El Kenno' - A Jealous God (Joshua 24:19)

Elohe Ma'ozi - God of My Strength (Psalm 43:2)

Elohim Machaseh Lanu - God Our Refuge (Psalm 62:8)

Eli Malekhi - God My King (Psalm 68:24)

El Marom - God Most High (Psalm 57:2)

El Nakamoth - God that Avengeth (Psalm 18:47)

El Nose' - God that Forgave (Psalm 99:8)

Elohenu 'Olam - The Everlasting God (Psalm 48:14)

Elohim 'Ozer Li - God My Helper (Psalm 54:4)

El Ra'i - Thou God Seest Me (Genesis 16:13)

El Sela - God, My Rock (Psalm 42:9)

El Shaddai - The Almighty God (Genesis 17:1,2)

Elohim Shephtim Ba'arets - God that Judgeth in the Earth (Psalm 58:11)

El Simchath Gili - God My Exceeding Joy (Psalm 43:4)

Elohim Tseba'oth - God of Hosts (Psalm 80:7)

Elohe Tishu'athi - God of my Salvation (Psalm 18:46; 51:14)

Elohe Tsadeki - God of my Righteousness (Psalm 4:1)

Elohe Ya'akob - God of Jacob (Psalm 20:1; 46:7)

Elohe Yisra'el - God of Israel (Psalm 59:5)

Total - 32

THE NAME OF JEHOVAH IN SCRIPTURE

Jehovah - The Lord (Exodus 6:2,3)

THE NAMES OF JESUS

Adonai Jehovah - The Lord God (Genesis 15:2)

Jehovah Adon Kal Ha'arets - The Lord, the Lord of All the Earth (Joshua 3:13)

Jehovah Bara - The Lord Creator (Isaiah 40:28)

Jehovah Chatsahi - The Lord My Strength (Psalm 27:1)

Jehovah Chereb - The Lord . . . the Sword (Deuteronomy 33:29)

Jehovah Eli - The Lord My God (Psalm 18:2)

Jehovah Elyon - The Lord Most High (Psalm 38:2)

Jehovah 'Ez-Lami - The Lord My Strength (Psalm 28:7)

Jehovah Gador Milchamah - The Lord Mighty in Battle (Psalm 24:8)

Jehovah Ganan - The Lord Our Defence (Psalm 89:18)

Jehovah Go'el - The Lord Thy Redeemer (Isaiah 49:26; 60:16)

Jehovah Hashopet - The Lord the Judge (Judges 6:27)

Jehovah Hoshe'ah - The Lord Save (Psalm 20:9)

Jehovah 'Immeku - The Lord Is with you (Judges 6:12)

Jehovah 'Izoz Hakaboth - The Lord Strong and Mighty (Psalm 24:8)

Jehovah Jireh - The Lord Will Provide (Genesis 22:14)

Jehovah Kabodhi - The Lord My Glory (Psalm 3:3)

Jehovah Kanna - The Lord Whose Name Is Jealous (Exodus 34:14)

Jehovah Keren-Yish'i - The Lord the Horn of My Salvation (Psalm 18:2)

Jehovah Machsi - The Lord My Refuge (Psalm 91:9)

Jehovah Magen - The Lord, the Shield (Deuteronomy 33:29)

Jehovah Ma'oz - The Lord . . . My Fortress (Jeremiah 16:19)

Hamelech Jehovah - The Lord the King (Psalm 98:6)

Jehovah Melech 'Olam - The Lord King Forever (Psalm 10:16)

Jehovah Mephalti - The Lord My Deliverer (Psalm 18:2)

Jehovah M'gaddishcem - The Lord Our Sanctifier (Exodus 31:13)

Jehovah Metsodhathi - The Lord . . . My Fortress (Psalm 18:2)

Jehovah Misqabbi - The Lord My High Tower (Psalm 18:2)
Jehovah Naheh - The Lord that Smiteth (Ezekiel 7:9)
Jehovah Nissi - The Lord Our Banner (Exodus 17:15)
Jehovah 'Ori - The Lord My Light (Psalm 27:1)
Jehovah Rapha - The Lord that Healeth (Exodus 15:26)
Jehovah Rohi - The Lord My Shepherd (Psalm 23:1)
Jehovah Sabaoth - The Lord of Hosts (I Samuel 1:3)
Jehovah Sel'i - The Lord My Rock (Psalm 18:2)
Jehovah Shalom - The Lord Our Peace (Judges 6:24)
Jehovah Shammah - The Lord Is There (Ezekiel 48:35)
Jehovah Tiskenu - The Lord Our Righteousness (Jeremiah 23:6)
Jehovah Tsori - O Lord My Strength (Psalm 19:14)
Jehovah 'Uzam - The Lord Their Strength (Psalm 37:39)
Jehovah Yasha - The Lord Thy Saviour (Isaiah 49:26; 60:16)

Total - 42

A SELECTED BIBLIOGRAPHY ON THE NAMES OF CHRIST

Hahn, Ferdinand. *The Titles of Jesus in Christology: Their History in Early Christianity.* Tr. Harold Knight and George Ogg. Cleveland, Ohio: The World Publishing Company, 1969.

Hausherr, Irenee. *The Name of Jesus.* Tr. Charles Cummings. Kalamazoo, Michigan: Cistercian Publications Inc., 1978.

Hill, Rowley. *52 Sermon Outlines on the Titles of Our Lord.* Grand Rapids, Michigan: Baker Book House, 1958.

Horton, T. C. and Hurlburt, Charles E. *The Wonderful Names of Our Wonderful Lord.* Los Angeles: Grant Publishing House, 1925.

Keller, W. Phillip. *A Layman Looks at the Lamb of God.* Minneapolis, Minnesota: Bethany House Publishers, 1982.

Krumwiede, Walter. *Names of Jesus: A Practical and Devotional Study of Some of the Names of Jesus.* Philadelphia: The United Lutheran Publication House, 1927.

Large, James. *Two Hundred and Eighty Titles and Symbols of Christ.* Grand Rapids, Michigan: Baker Book House, 1959.

Lee, Robert. *Similies of Our Lord and "His Own" or Bible Word Pictures of our Lord and of the Christian.* London: Pickering & Inglis, n.d.

Lockyer, Herbert. "The Greatest of All Bible Men, Jesus Christ," in *All the Men of the Bible.* Grand Rapids, Michigan: Zondervan Publishing House, 1958.

Rolls, Charles J. *The Indescribable Christ: The Names and Titles of Jesus Christ.* Grand Rapids, Michigan: Zondervan Publishing House, 1953.

Rolls, Charles J. *The World's Greatest Name: The Names and Titles of Jesus Christ.* Grand Rapids, Michigan: Zondervan Publishing House, 1956.

Rolls, Charles J. *Time's Noblest Name: The Names and Titles of Jesus Christ (L Through O)*. Grand Rapids, Michigan: Zondervan Publishing House, 1958.

Rolls, Charles J. *The Name Above Every Name: The Names and Titles of Jesus Christ (P. Q. R. S.)*. Neptune, New Jersey: Loizeaux Brothers, 1965.

Rolls, Charles J. *His Glorious Names: The Names and Titles of Jesus Christ (T. U. V. W.)*. Neptune, New Jersey: Loizeaux Brothers, 1975.

Spurgeon, Charles Haddon. *Sermons on Christ's Names and Titles*. Ed. Charles T. Cook. Grand Rapids, Michigan: Zondervan Publishing House, 1961.

Stevenson, Herbert F. *Titles of the Triune God: Studies in Divine Self-Revelation*. Westwood, New Jersey: Fleming H. Revell Company, 1956.

Taylor, Vincent. *The Names of Jesus*. London: Macmillan and Co., Limited, 1953.

Warfield, Benjamin B. *The Lord of Glory: A Study of the Designations of Our Lord in the New Testament with Especial Reference to His Deity*. Grand Rapids, Michigan: Baker Book House, 1976.